GOOD ENOUGH?

Romans 12:1-2

Jeff Mikels

GOOD ENOUGH?

God, Sinners & Salvation in the Book of Romans

Jeff Kliewer

Editing by Jeanette Windle, JM Windle Manuscript Services

Cover by Kelli Campbell, kellicdesign

Interior Layout by Tricia Lippincott

ISBN: 0692429980
ISBN 13: 9780692429983
Library of Congress Control Number: 2015939500
Faith House Publishers, Mt. Laurel, NJ

Contents

Introduction

In the 1998 film *Saving Private Ryan*, an elderly James Ryan cries at the graveside of Captain Miller, who fell in a WW2 effort to rescue him. Three of Ryan's brothers had already been killed in combat, so a group of soldiers led by Captain Miller set out to save their desperate mother's last surviving son. Like many of his men, Captain Miller died on the mission to save Ryan, but not before encountering Private Ryan and uttering two dying words to him: "Earn this."

As the elderly Ryan stands at the grave of Captain Miller, he reflects back upon his life and is troubled by the question of whether or not he earned the right to live after the war. He knows that men died in order that he might live, but he doesn't know whether or not he proceeded to live a good enough life to warrant the sacrifice that others made for him. Private Ryan lived out his days after the war under the weight of a crushing question: Am I good enough?

Like Private Ryan, each of us needs to consider whether or not our lives are good enough. Am I good enough? A weighty question like this can only be answered if we know certain things about God, sinners, and salvation. Is God good enough to vanquish evil? Can a sinner like me ever be good enough to stand in the presence of a Holy God? Is the message of salvation in Jesus Christ good enough to warrant my trust and allegiance? These are the questions of life. Who is "good enough"? What is "good enough"?

As for God, how good is He? We already know He must be strong. Isn't He the One that lined up galaxies one after another like a child turns out coloring pages and tapes them to the wall? Yet He deals so delicately with His creation that thousands of optic nerves spring out from behind tiny eyes as God forms a baby in a womb. Each microscopic nerve will have to find its unique mate from the thousands of nerves that arise from the brain stem. When we behold the distant stars, it is only because our optic nerves made their connections. We can only see because God was good enough to give us eyes to see. God must really care about us. Why then do our eyes also have to see so much evil?

God is strong. God is good. But evil is all around. So is God good enough? That is a burning question.

As for us, how good are we? We are so weak that we often give in to the smallest of temptations. We are astonishingly swift to run after anything that promises to please us, to make us happy or accepted or significant. But we are painfully slow to turn our eyes up toward heaven, to contemplate what truly pleases God. We often live like little gods and ignore the voice of conscience that we know must come from God. We can admit that we have overstepped some boundaries. So how many good deeds do we need to pile onto the scales of God's justice in order to balance out the bad deeds we have done? How much good do we have to do in order to be good enough for God?

If we compare ourselves with others, we may judge ourselves to be okay. But God alone will be our Judge. Are we good enough? That is a burning question. ✍

As for salvation, how good is it? We have heard Christians preach a message called "the gospel", meaning good news. It is told that Jesus Christ is the Son of God who died on a cross and rose from the dead to save us from our sins. The message has proven strong enough to run around the world. From the country with the largest number of Christians per capita (possibly South Korea) to the countries with the smallest number (probably many of the countries nearest to Israel), "the gospel" seems to be running faster than ever. Only a small percentage of all the people in this world can claim that they have never heard anything of the Christian message of salvation. But hearing and believing are two separate things. Many people who hear, perhaps most, will never believe. So is the message of salvation in Jesus Christ really good enough for the world? Is it good enough for you and me?

There are billions of people on the planet who either don't know or don't believe the message of salvation. Is "the gospel" good enough? That is a burning question.

I see the answers to these burning questions and many other related questions in the pages of a book. It is really a letter that a man named Paul wrote around the year 56 AD, but it has come to be known as the book of Romans. When I read Romans, the words do not come to me like those in an ordinary book. To me, it is as though the book of Romans opens my eyes to see the truth, not by merely relaying information from the printed page through my optic nerves to be processed in my brain, but by actually giving me new eyes with which to see. It shows me the answers to the questions of who and what are *good enough*, and it changes my life in so doing.

I believe that the words of Romans themselves are infused with God's power to open our eyes. So in this book *Good Enough?*, I present the book of Romans in its entirety, along with my own comments derived from careful study and personal encounter with the text. I consider it my role to make comments that simplify, explain, and expound upon the book of Romans. An ordinary person—a sinner just like us—wrote the book. But as you read what he wrote, I hope you will come to agree with me that behind the scenes God Himself has clearly inspired Paul's words. That is how the book of Romans came to be included in the Bible, and that is why sinners like us desperately need to hear what it says.

The different books that make up the Bible each play different roles in communicating what God has to say to humanity. Some recount history and bring perspective to the man who is searching for his place in this world. Others recite poetry and stir the soul of the one who looks for beauty and longs for joy in a world where suffering is inevitable. Sixty-six books play a thousand different roles. But one book among them—the book of Romans—is assigned the profound duty of carefully stating the main thing that God wants to say to humanity, and it does so masterfully. Romans is a book every sinner needs to read.

Even the most skeptical non-Christian literature professors in the leading academic institutions in the world will not deny that Romans is a literary masterpiece. But the great men and women *of faith*, who have been reading this book ever since it was written, all seem to agree that the book of Romans is more than that. Many consider it the most profound book ever written.

It is the book that binds the Bible together. All that went before Romans culminates in the historical accounts of the life, death, burial, and resurrection of Jesus Christ and the subsequent birth of the church that bears His Name. The book of Romans awaits directly after Matthew, Mark, Luke, John, and Acts tell the greatest stories ever told. The reader approaches it asking questions. What does all this mean? How does the story of Jesus apply to me? What must I do to be saved? How does Jesus impact my life? All Scripture has power to bring sinners to salvation, but Romans is precisely geared to this one most important agenda.

Bringing sinners to salvation is what the book of Romans has been doing for two thousand years. When controversies began to erupt in the fourth century church, God used the book of Romans to convert the hedonist Augustine and raise him up as a theological captain to right the ship, steering the church to preach a pure message of salvation. When in the Middle Ages, the light of the church had dimmed and priests went about the countryside offering to sell God's forgiveness (in order to raise money for Vatican building projects), God steered the eyes of a young priest named Martin Luther to the book of Romans. Learning what it means that "the just shall live by faith" (Romans 1:17), Luther went on to lead the Protestant Reformation, which brought many millions to faith in Christ. Many of those Protestants like John Wesley, founder of the Methodist church, first came to have their hearts "strangely warmed" by reading the book of Romans. Even today, all over the world, the book of Romans is leading people to salvation.

Romans is a theological masterpiece that lays out the plan of salvation in perfect order. It meets a sinner like me at the point of need and carries the sinner to the place of forgiveness. Having gotten the sinner saved, it doesn't then abandon the newborn saint to return like a swine to wallow in the mud of sin. Rather it illuminates the path for the saint to walk upon and thus arrive safely home.

Romans cannot be improved upon. Why then would a sinner like me feel compelled to comment on its verses? I did so for the same reason that God gave the book in the first place. In every generation, God sends certain saints to help sinners walk the *Romans Road.* Saints are nothing but sinners who have already walked the road. All of us who believe in Jesus are saints. No one has to be a Christian rock star to get that title, and the pronouncements of those who teach the contrary mean nothing. Just as every believer in Jesus is a saint, so every saint can potentially teach others the meaning of the book of Romans. But in the church, God sends certain ones—call them preachers and teachers, nothing more—to communicate the meaning of the text in terms that listeners can understand. The book of Romans speaks for itself. I write to shine a light upon it.

Every sinner is lost in the jungle of sin and blind to the Truth. God gave the book of Romans to provide a roadmap out of the jungle and into eternal life. Romans opens our eyes to the Truth. It has seven sections, each one revealing a key truth that builds upon the previous one. If our lives in this world can be compared to those of slaves in the ancient city of Rome, then going through the seven sections of the book of Romans is like traversing the Seven Hills of Rome to escape Roman captivity and enter the freedom of the City of God.

As you travel on the *Romans Road,* the road that brings sinners out of slavery in Rome to the celestial city where God has His home, you will find yourself healed of blindness. If you read Romans with an open heart, by its end your eyes will have opened to see clearly everything that matters most. But each progressive step on the road is necessary. One must make it through Rome, rejecting her deceptions, as the book of Romans brings light to bear upon this city of man. The book of Romans takes the reader out of Rome and further away from Rome every time the traveler traverses its pages. It brings us nearer and nearer to the Source of the Light. The Light that shines is the Word of God.

The written word reveals the living person—Jesus Christ—not only by conveying information to our brains, but by imparting vision to our souls. God opens the eyes of our hearts through the instrument of His word. This is how spiritual sight is restored to us—blind sinners—and how sinners like us make it out of the jungle of sin. God can use Romans in every sinner's life to open eyes to the truth and set the captive free.

God has not abandoned us here to be consumed by the fire of life's burning questions. Is God good enough to deserve my trust and devotion? Am I good enough to deserve His acceptance? Is the message of salvation good enough to save completely? God gave us the book of Romans to answer these important questions. Moreover, God gave the book of Romans as an instrument through which He offers eternal life to sinners who need saving.

SECTION 1

The Way to be Good with God
Romans 1:1-17

1

Destination

"Paul, a bond-servant of Christ Jesus, called as an
apostle, set apart for the gospel of God"

—*Romans 1:1*

In order to use a Map App on my Smart Phone, I need to enter a starting point and a destination. Before I hit "start" and that female voice starts telling me which way to go, the App shows me an overview of the route. It helps to see the big picture before thinking about particular turns. If I can understand the big idea of where I'm going, I'm less likely to get lost in the details. This principle applies to many things. A good book or speech needs a thesis statement that lays out the main idea before the content of the book or speech begins to make points related to that thesis. It helps to see an overview.

The book of Romans is true to form. Its opening verses, Romans 1:1-17, are devoted to identifying the author and the subjects to whom he writes. But more than that, we are given an overview of the route that *every sinner* needs to travel.

Continuing with this travel analogy, we can conceive of ourselves as being on a journey. The book of Romans is our map, and the first 17 verses are an overview of our route. We start at an isolated place, disconnected from God. Our destination is the point of being well established in a right relationship with God, saved from our sins and genuinely living by faith. The end point of our journey is to be good with God.

Faith, we will discover, is the only thing we bring to the journey along the *Romans Road*. But even faith is not something we muster up. It is the response of our hearts to the truth of God as He reveals it to us. Faith is what prompts the steps of a traveler as he knowingly walks where the map tells him to go.

The Way is certainly not something that we can make up. We *must* follow God's map. Faith is worthless if it isn't placed in a fitting object. If all roads lead to Rome, the same is not true of the Way to the City of God. All other roads do lead back to Rome, the city of man, the home of sinners separated from a Holy God. The book of Romans shows us the path that we must follow, not a trail that we must blaze or a man-made road back to Rome. The first verse of our roadmap (the first verse in the book of Romans) gives God's road a name. The road is called "the gospel". We need this road to eternal life.

The *gospel* is the thesis of the book of Romans. It is the overview on our Map App. But what is the gospel? Simply put, the gospel is the good news that Jesus Christ is the Son of God who died and rose from the dead in order that all who trust in Him will have their sins forgiven and will have eternal life. This is the simple message that falls from the lips of every genuine Christian on the planet. The book of Romans proclaims this simple message, and not only so, it sets out to address the most profound *implications* that arise from such news as this. The book of Romans tells us how to become a Christian and how to live as one. The big idea of the book is a call to a genuine life of faith in the gospel. Romans 1:1-17 provides a big-picture overview of this life.

1:1   Paul, a bond-servant of Christ Jesus, called as an
               apostle, set apart for the gospel of God

The first verse identifies the human author of the book of Romans. His name was *Paul*, in Greek, although Saul was his Hebrew name. He wrote half of the New Testament, which means that Paul is one of the most widely read authors in history. His missionary efforts carried the gospel across the Roman Empire, crossing even the most difficult divide, the line between Jew and Gentile. His conversion exemplifies the power of the gospel. The hater of all Christians whose very mission was to persecute the church becomes one of the church's greatest Christian leaders. After conversion, his impeccable life becomes an example for all generations of

Christians to follow (Philippians 3:17, 1 Corinthians 11:1). He endures incredible suffering, not counting his own life too dear to him, for the sake of advancing the gospel. He ultimately gives his life, dying a martyr's death in the very city to which the book of Romans was written years earlier.

By what title should we remember such a Christian leader as this? Shall we call him "Priest"? Shall we call him "Bishop of Rome"? Is he to be our beloved "Vicar of Christ"? Dare we say "Alter Christos"—*Another Christ*? Would it be right for us to call him "Pope", derived from the Latin *papa*, meaning "Father"? Would we even apply the title "*Holy* Father" to him? Should we even shine the spotlight upon him at all?

Paul would have none of it! After giving his name, Paul gives the title by which he wanted to be remembered—"*a bond-servant of Christ Jesus*". Paul identified himself as a δοῦλος in the Greek (transliterated to English as "doulos"), meaning "slave", by which term he meant to relinquish all his rights except that of belonging to Jesus Christ: Here was a man who felt so indebted to his Savior that he considered his life to be given completely over to Christ's control. Paul's very identity—the way Paul saw himself as a person—was wrapped up in his relationship with Jesus Christ.

This, dear reader, is the destination. This is where Paul, by the preaching of his gospel, would like to bring us. This is where the Romans Road is able to take us. To be so entirely devoted to Jesus Christ that one can say, "For to me, to live is Christ" (Philippians 1:21), is what it means to be really alive. Eternal life, it turns out, begins before physical death. We come alive as soon as we meet Jesus Christ. The more He increases in us and we decrease in ourselves, the more life we experience. The autonomous person that we are, living for whatever motivates us, living under the control of our own human reasoning, is not actually alive at all.

Paul does not see himself as an autonomous person. He is controlled by Another. He is motivated by the cause of Another. He reasons with the mind of Another. His very identity is in submission to the Lord of his life. Death is not the end for a man like this. "To die is gain" (Philippians 1:21) if it brings us into the very presence of the One who owns us, the One we love with an undying love (Ephesians 6:24). So, dying to self is the destination. To be so completely alive to Jesus Christ that we consider ourselves nothing but His slave is the destination of the Romans Road, the place where the gospel alone can take us.

In verse 1, we learn that Paul is "a bond-servant", or *slave*, to Christ Jesus. The way Paul identifies himself is an example for us to follow. If we, like him, can identify ourselves this way, not simply with lip service but as a reflection of what is true about ourselves, then we also have the life that Paul experienced. The gospel will have done its work in us.

Next in verse 1, after identifying himself in submission to Christ, Paul mentions his role in the church, that of *"an apostle"*. The Greek word for apostle (ἀπόστολος—"apostolos") means "sent one". So, what is Paul sent to do? He is set apart and sent out to preach *"the gospel of God"*. This is his calling, or mission, and it is reflected in the term *apostle*.

But *apostle* is not only a missionary term. It is also a special designation that Christ Himself applied to his twelve disciples (Matthew 10:2-4, Mark 3:14, Luke 6:13, Acts 1:13). When Paul identifies himself as an apostle, he says something about the authority of the words he is about to give. He claims a level of authority that equals that of the twelve.

Along with a few others who were later designated as apostles[1], the twelve (all of whom were eyewitnesses of the resurrection) were charged with laying the foundation of the church (Ephesians 2:20). That included the writing of the New Testament. The Apostle Peter wrote two of those books. At the end of the second, he recognized Paul's writings as "Scriptures" (2 Peter 3:16). Peter knew that other people would try to distort, twist and pervert what Paul had written, or ignore it altogether, and would do so to their own destruction. But as an apostle, Peter affirmed that Paul's writings were to be regarded as *Scripture*.

The importance of apostolic authority needs to be underscored. Contrary to modern lies about the church deciding what books to include in the New Testament hundreds of years later (after the Council of Nicea in 325 AD, it is usually alleged), the church always recognized the Scriptures that the apostles wrote or supervised. Paul wrote the book of Romans. He was an apostle, so the book is stamped with God's approval.

From verse 1, we learn that Paul understood that he was writing authoritatively as an *apostle* of God. At the same time, he kept a humble attitude that identified himself as a *slave* of Jesus Christ, an attitude that we also would do well to desire to have. We should ask God to bring us to this destination in our own lives. This destination is available to us if we follow the road marked out for us in the *gospel*, to which Paul turns his attention in the next verse.

---

[1] In Acts 1:26, Matthias replaced the traitor, Judas Iscariot, returning the number of apostles to 12. Later, we learn that a few others, like Barnabas (Acts 14:14), Silas and Timothy (1 Thessalonians 2:6 with 1:1), are called by that title.

2

Gospel

"which He promised beforehand through His
prophets in the holy Scriptures"

—*Romans 1:2*

We have learned that the destination to which the book of Romans seeks to bring us is the freedom of being willingly enslaved to our Maker. Since God made us, we are only at home with Him when the proper relationship between Creator and created being has been reestablished. In order to bring us there, God commissioned Paul to write the book of Romans. In the first verse, Paul introduced himself as a bond-servant of Christ, an apostle, and a preacher of the gospel. In the next three verses, he will introduce the gospel itself. The rest of the book of Romans will unfold the layers of meaning that is contained in the gospel. But by way of introduction, we are immediately given the grounds for believing the gospel and some of the foundational content of it.

1:2   which He promised beforehand through His prophets
in the holy Scriptures

That it was *"promised beforehand"* is Paul's first thought about *the gospel*, so this verse is important and worthy of our careful consideration. In tracking with Paul's sentence, it would be easy to skim past verse 2, because it is something of an aside. But this phrase needed to be inserted because it mirrors a pressing concern that we find throughout the New Testament.

The New Testament authors constantly referenced the Old Testament. That which was accomplished in the life, death and resurrection of Jesus Christ was thoroughly disclosed *ahead of time* in the Old Testament. When Matthew wrote his New Testament book, he quoted the Old Testament more than sixty times. Mark starts his Gospel with an Old Testament quote. Luke draws his Gospel to a close with Jesus' reminder "that all things which are written about Me in the Law of Moses and the Prophets and the Psalms must be fulfilled" (Luke 24:44). John is sure to include Jesus saying, "You search the Scriptures because you think that in them you have eternal life; it is these that testify about Me" (John 5:39). All the New Testament authors are like Matthew, Mark, Luke and John in recognizing the importance of the fact that Jesus fulfilled the Old Testament prophecies about a coming Messiah.

Paul understood the gospel to be "that Christ died for our sins according to the Scriptures, and that He was buried, and that He was raised on the third day according to the Scriptures" (1 Corinthians 15:3-4). Notice that the basis for believing the message is its consistency with what was previously written in the Old Testament ("according to the Scriptures"). That is why the gospel *requires* the obedience of faith (Romans 1:5).

Think about that. On what basis are people required to believe in a Person and Work that they have never seen? How can God hold people eternally responsible for believing or not believing in Jesus Christ if we have never seen Him? We didn't see Him on the cross. We didn't see Him resurrected three days later.

The requirement of faith in Jesus Christ is right and just, because *faith* is taking God at His Word, and His Word sufficiently testifies to the Person and Work of Jesus Christ. Many people wrongly believe that faith is a blind leap. In reality, faith is the proper response to the revelation of Truth. When God speaks, it is correct and fitting that we believe what He says. And God has so spoken. He spoke in a way that only He can. "I, even I, am the Lord, and there is no savior besides Me. It is I who have declared and saved and proclaimed" (Isaiah 43:11-12a). Only God can declare the future and then bring it to pass precisely as He promised. He promised to come and save us. When He did it, the world was accountable to believe

Him. Salvation through Jesus Christ is even now being declared and proclaimed. The message is based on the Holy Scriptures.

Where then are the prophecies in the Old Testament that specifically proclaim the death and resurrection of Jesus? The place of His birth is foretold in Micah 5:2. That He would be born to a virgin is prophesied in Isaiah 7:14. Every book of the Old Testament prophetically reveals Jesus Christ in one way or another. But where specifically is it promised that the Messiah would die for our sins and rise from the dead? Where is "the gospel of God" (Romans 1:1) "promised beforehand through His prophets in the holy Scriptures" (Romans 1:2)? Paul does not say here in Romans 1:2, but from reviewing the Old Testament, here is my top ten list of the Scriptures that Paul likely had in mind.

1.	Isaiah 53	Details of the death and victory of a substitute.
2.	Psalm 22	Jesus cites Psalm 22 while dying in like fashion.
3.	Leviticus 17:11	Shedding of innocent blood to atone for sin.
4.	Psalm 110	The Lord is like Melchizedek of Genesis 14.
5.	Genesis 22	Abraham's near sacrifice of Isaac has patterns.
6.	Psalm 16	David's son won't suffer decay after death.
7.	Exodus 12	The death of the Passover Lamb foreshadows.
8.	Numbers 21	The bronze serpent raised on a pole symbolizes.
9.	Zechariah 12:10	Israel looks on Him whom they pierced.
10.	Deut. 21:23	One bears the curse by being hanged on a tree.

The presence of even the first of these prophecies provides reason enough to believe the gospel. That we have these ten and many more (Genesis 3:15, Zechariah 13:6) renders the case conclusive. These specifically speak of Messiah's death and resurrection, which is the core message of the gospel.

There is absolutely no doubt that each of these prophecies was recorded no less than four hundred years prior to the birth of Jesus[2]. There is also little use in disputing the claim that Jesus Christ fulfilled them. When you explore the details of Jesus' crucifixion and realize that the prophets mentioned such minute details as when the soldiers "divide my garments among them, and for my clothing they cast lots" (Psalm 22:18)

---

[2] The Hebrew Bible (what became the Christian Old Testament) was translated into different languages and dispersed throughout the world long before Jesus came. The discovery of the Dead Sea Scrolls in 1948 gave us actual copies that date back to prior to the time of Jesus. The Dead Sea Scrolls had portions of virtually every Old Testament book. There was even a scroll containing the entire Book of Isaiah.

or when "they pierced my hands and my feet" (Psalm 22:16), you realize that there are far too many details to chalk up to coincidence. Since David, the author of Psalm 22, wrote five hundred years before crucifixion was even invented, there is no reason to doubt that what he wrote was nothing short of prophetic. Isaiah can prove the case on his own.

> *"But He was pierced through for our transgressions, He was crushed for our iniquities; the chastening for our well-being fell upon Him, and by His scourging we are healed. All of us like sheep have gone astray, each of us have turned to his own way, but the Lord has caused the iniquity of us all to fall upon Him" (Isaiah 53:5-6)*

Isaiah wrote these words more than seven hundred years before Jesus was crucified. In so doing, he gave the reason for the crucifixion. Since that reason is precisely the same as the gospel that all genuine Christians preach, the point is established. What more should God have said, given that He was speaking *ahead of time*? God "promised beforehand through His prophets in the holy Scriptures" (Romans 1:2). God always remains consistent. The only question is whether or not each of us will believe what He says. But Paul's first point about the gospel, that it is according to the Old Testament, is supported by very strong evidence.

1:3-4   concerning His Son, who was born of a descendant of
                David according to the flesh, who was declared the
                Son of God with power by the resurrection from the
                dead, according to the Spirit of holiness, Jesus Christ
                our Lord

Paul's first point provided the ground upon which the gospel is built, so now he is ready to begin the construct that rises from that foundation. Certainly "the holy Scriptures" (Romans 1:2) make a sure foundation, but not everyone builds there. Even to this day, people are constantly constructing messages they call "gospel" that are not supported by the Scriptures. These teachers fancy themselves capable of telling others what God is like. They presume to speak for Him, telling others the news that they call *good*. But the authoritative *gospel* that Paul constructs, relayed to the world from God through an apostle and having its foundation in the Old Testament, has certain distinct properties.

First, the gospel of God concerns Jesus Christ, as we see in verse 3: "concerning His Son". No other religious figure nor a concept of man can ever take the place of Jesus the Nazarene. If someone proposes another object of faith, it is a foreign substance. It does not belong in the gospel. The gospel concerns Jesus.

Second, notice that He eternally exists in unity with two other eternally existent Persons. There cannot be One called "*Son of God*" unless there is a Father. The Father is typically referred to only as "*God*." And then, there is also a third mentioned—"*the Spirit of holiness*" or Holy Spirit. These three Persons are so unified that at first glance when reading Romans 1:3-4, it appears that there is only one subject of the sentence. Indeed there is. Jesus Christ is the One who occupies that place in the sentence. But His unity with the Father and Spirit is evidently so complete that each is mentioned in association with Him. Jesus, His Father, and His Spirit belong intrinsically together.

In Romans 1:3-4, Paul is not intending to expound upon the concept of the Trinity (Jesus already did that, later to be recorded in the book of John, chapters 14-16). Paul mentions all three Persons only as a matter of course. Paul simply *accepts* the Trinity. It thus follows that anyone who denies the Trinity, that is, the Tri-Unity or Three-in-Oneness of God, has necessarily denied the gospel and replaced the genuine with a counterfeit. The Trinity is intrinsic to the gospel.

Third, there is a deliberate statement of the humanity of Jesus. With false preachers following prophets of their own liking, it is helpful that Paul identifies the real historical human figure that is the Object of His gospel. The Son of God "was born of a descendant of David" (1:3). In Greek, the word "descendant" (σπέρμα) transliterates as "sperma" and refers to the "seed" of David. Mary was descended physically from David, and so was that first Son born from her body. Jesus' descent from David is "according to the flesh," which underscores the real humanity of the Son. This clearly identifiable man is the one true Object of saving faith. If it is *the gospel* you want, no one else will do.

Fourth, there are also three explicit declarations of the *Deity* of Jesus. First, although fully human, Jesus is here called the "Son of God." Because He demonstrated unprecedented power when he conquered death, His identity is revealed to be so much more than human. But how different is Jesus compared to every other human who has ever lived? The term "Son of God" refers to His utterly unique nature. As a Son, He shares the very nature of His Father, who is said here to be God. Nowhere in the Bible is the Son of God said to have been generated or procreated in any way by the Father. Rather, the eternal relationship between the Two is described to us in terms that we can understand. It is the relationship between a Father and His one and only Son.

When Jesus Christ walked here among us, His feet got dirty, but never with the mud of sin. Whenever a temptation came after Him, He utterly defeated it. His life was literally sinless. How could this be true of a human, given what we all observe of human nature? No one else we know is perfect in every way, all the time. Jesus walked in the "*Spirit of holiness*" because He was God, and therefore by nature holy all the time. This, the holiness in which He walked, proves that He was in a perfect unity with the Holy Spirit. It is the second indication in Romans 1:4 that Jesus is God.

The third indication is the title Paul gives to Jesus—κύριος (Kurios), meaning "Lord." When referring not to an earthly master, such as a slave owner or person of respect, but to the King of Heaven, κύριος is a term that must mean God. Part of becoming a Christian is acknowledging with one's mouth and heart that Jesus is the Lord of all (Romans 10:9). That means acknowledging His full deity, because the Greek word for God (θεός, Theos) is not given a higher rank than κύριος. In places like Romans 14:6, the two words are used almost interchangeably. There is never any indication of the subordination of "Lord" to "God," but the Lord God is called both.

So, we learn from verses 3-4 that Jesus Christ is the second member of the Trinity. He is fully human and also fully divine. He is the Object of faith presented to us in the gospel. The gospel is the message about Him.

3

Grace

*"through whom we have received grace and apostleship
to bring about the obedience of faith among all the
Gentiles for His name's sake"*

—*Romans 1:5*

The Road Map to eternal life has already been simply stated in three short verses. It is the message about Jesus Christ (who He is and what He has done). It is grounded in Old Testament prophecy, which is what makes the claim believable. But if believing the gospel were only a matter of being told these simple truths, then the book of Romans could stop right here. As it turns out, many long chapters remain, because although the gospel is simple enough to reach the heart of a child, it is not simplistic.

The gospel holds an inexhaustible storehouse of treasures that manifest themselves as a person digs deeper and deeper into the gospel. The trouble is that none of us would be willing to dig if we were left to our own devices. We may feign an effort to understand the gospel, but our hearts are too distractible to really go all out. We might even read through Romans, but the eyes of our hearts would still be unable to see the glorious light that is in the face of Christ (2 Corinthians 4:4). When it comes to spiritual things, reading comprehension is not so much a matter of intelligence as it is a matter of the heart.

The key to receiving spiritual blessings from God, even to truly understand His word, is the present activity of God in our hearts. We actually cannot even seek after God unless He first draws us to it. We are utterly dependent on God's kindness working in our lives in order to receive anything good, and the good thing is, it is according to His nature to be good to us. We have a word for this kindness that God extends to undeserving sinners like us. It is the key to understanding the gospel: *grace*.

1:5-6   through whom we have received grace and apostleship
                to bring about the obedience of faith among all the
                Gentiles for His name's sake, among whom you also
                are the called of Jesus Christ

Even as Paul continues to introduce his own role in verses 5-6, he keeps the spotlight and focus upon the One who sent him. Jesus Christ was the Object of attention in verses 1-4. We learned that Paul is *Jesus'* slave, set apart for a lifelong mission of preaching *Jesus*. We heard that the gospel is based in the Old Testament, which put the spotlight on *Jesus* even before He came. We saw that the content of the gospel is *Jesus*—a real human who really is the Son of God and Lord of all. Now in verse 5, Paul needs to say why he is writing to the Romans, but he simply refuses to spotlight himself. Rather, he wants all glory to be given to the Son. So, if Paul is the apostle to the Gentiles, it is only because he has "received" unprecedented "grace" from God the Father *through Jesus Christ*.

Grace, χάρις (charis), is God's favorable disposition in extending Himself toward a person in order to show them kindness. God leans in to bless a man because that is what He has within Himself to do. It doesn't depend on the person that God chooses to so favor. Grace comes from God's nature. Since the fullest expression of God's nature *is* the Person Jesus Christ, it is fitting that the grace that Paul claims to have received comes "through" (1:5) "Jesus Christ our Lord" (1:4). The Father and Son therefore deserve the glory for making Paul an apostle to the Gentiles. The apostle reaffirms this. He has already said that his apostleship is owed to God's grace. Now he reiterates that the result of his ministry is "for His [Jesus'] name's sake" (1:5). Let all the glory go to the name above every name—*Jesus Christ*.

Let the nations of the world *obey* God's command to believe in Him. Paul seeks to "bring about the obedience of faith" (1:5). Notice that even though "gospel" simply means "good news," God requires something of those who hear it. The news is good, so no one should complain. But there is a right response to the revelation of God's Truth. Paul calls it the *obedience* of faith. And where there is the expectation of obedience, there is also the possibility of disobedience. Not every Gentile in the world will believe in Jesus. Some will hear the Truth and defiantly harden their hearts in opposition to God's message. But God Himself will see to it, by sending the apostle Paul and future generations of preachers who carry His apostolic message, that "*among* all the Gentiles" (1:5), some will be brought to the "*obedience of faith*" (1:5).

How it could be that *free will* plays into the number of those that *grace* brings to obedience, the text does not say here. But we are assured that God's *grace* will "bring about" the obedient faith of those who will believe. Since the possibility of there being *obedience* presupposes a *free will*, the concepts of *grace* and *free will* must not be mutually exclusive. In the end, God will surely bring a people to Himself, and those ultimately found outside of that number will have their own willful disobedience to blame.

The recipients of the book of Romans were mostly Gentiles (non-Jews). But the apostle to the Gentiles did not consider them second-class citizens in God's eyes. Sure, God called the descendants of Jacob to be His chosen people. And they will always be special under the unbreakable covenants He made with them. But there in Rome was a group of believers in Jesus who had joyfully obeyed the call to put their faith in Jesus. Paul says to them what also applies to any of us who are willing to believe the gospel. "You also are the called of Jesus Christ" (1:6). Herein is a privilege that is even greater than to be called an "Israelite." To be the "called of Jesus Christ" is to have received the greatest news of all. Someone has told you about Jesus Christ. You heard about who He is—the Son of the Living God—and what He did for you—died in your place and rose from the dead.

This message did not come to you as a dead religious message. Rather, your heart was also called by it. The external message penetrated through the gate of your ears as you heard or through your eyes as you read. But some internal force drew you to recognize that the message came from God Himself. It was a force at work inside of you, but not something that came from you. If you have received the message, in understanding it and in having been successfully drawn to believe it in your heart, then you are "the called of Jesus Christ". You owe it all to *grace*.

1:7   to all who are beloved of God in Rome, called as
             saints: Grace to you and peace from God our Father
             and the Lord Jesus Christ.

Paul now formally addresses his letter specifically to the Roman Christians. It is important to remember the dual nature of the Bible at this point. Just as Jesus—the personified "Word of God" (John 1:1)—has two natures (one fully human, the other fully divine), so also the Bible—the written "Word of God" (Psalm 119)—has two natures.

As the book of Romans was being written, it was fully the product of Paul's mind, written from this man to a particular people who lived in a real city at a certain time in history. As Jesus' body performed normally in functions of ordinary human life, so the book of Romans functioned normally as a letter giving insight and directives to the ordinary believers who lived in Rome. But when Jesus walked the earth, God dwelt unrecognized among men. So too did the word of Paul come to Rome with a second and more important nature. It was the very Word of God to all men. It takes different people various amounts of time to recognize it as such, but the Bible is inspired by God to the fullest. Paul addressed "the beloved of God in Rome," but at the same time, God speaks to all who are willing to listen.

Those who believe are "called as saints." The Greek construction of this phrase does not imply that God calls to Himself those who are holy enough to be counted worthy. The Greek for "saints" transliterates as *hagios*, which does in fact mean "holy." But the Greek equivalent for the English word "as" is just not there. Paul is actually saying that God has certain beloved ones, and they are called "saints." "*Saints*" is like a nickname God gives to His loved ones that tells us how He sees us. He remembers none of our sin. He looks at us as His holy ones. We are "beloved" and named "saints" even though we did nothing but believe the message by which we were called to Him.

Like the ordinary Christians at Rome, all Christians are loved and called saints. But how are we to receive any benefit from the blessing that Paul pronounces over his readers in Rome? "Grace to you and peace from God our Father and the Lord Jesus Christ." The Word of God comes to us just as the letter of Paul arrived in the believers' hands at Rome. As the Romans read this blessing and the epistle to which it serves as a benediction, grace and peace flowed from Almighty God. But what about us?

Today, many of us can pull up Romans on a smartphone with a few taps. We probably have our own personal copy of the Bible at home. I have many Bibles in many languages and multiple translations into English. Such things would be unthinkable to the first century church in Rome. They couldn't conceive of it. But we can imagine how much they valued that original letter from Paul. They made copies by hand and dispersed them throughout the Roman Empire. We are still discovering copies that were sent throughout the Empire. But our access does us no good if we do not avail ourselves of it. If only we will read the book of Romans, consider its meaning, and value it with our time more than we value our phones, TVs, computers, and other things of this world, then *grace* and *peace* will flow to us from God our Father and the Lord Jesus Christ.

4

Prayer

*"always in my prayers making request, if perhaps now at last
by the will of God I may succeed in coming to you"*

—*Romans 1:10*

The destination of the Romans Road is to be in right standing in the presence of Almighty God. We stand there as His bond-servants, and yet He calls us "friends" (John 15:15). For our part, service to Him is not burdensome (Matthew 11:30). To serve the One who saved us is our greatest joy and privilege. We are not slaves begrudgingly, but willingly. Our life in Christ is the farthest thing imaginable from empty religious rituals performed in dutiful but unwanted obedience to a master's commands. Our life in Christ is a relationship. Paul models for us what that life—that relationship with God—ought to look like.

1:8-13   First, I thank my God through Jesus Christ for you all, because your faith is being proclaimed throughout the whole world. For God, whom I serve in my spirit in the preaching of the gospel of His Son, is my witness as to how unceasingly I make mention of you, always in my prayers making request, if perhaps now at last

> by the will of God I may succeed in coming to you. For I long to see you so that I may impart some spiritual gift to you, that you may be established; that is, that I may be encouraged together with you while among you, each of us by the other's faith, both yours and mine. I do not want you to be unaware, brethren, that often I have planned to come to you (and have been prevented so far) so that I may obtain some fruit among you also, even as among the rest of the Gentiles.

When Paul says *first*, he does not mean that what he is about to say is the most important truth he would like the Romans to know. Rather, chronologically speaking, there is something that Paul wants the Roman believers to know *first*, as a preface before he launches into the meat of the theology that he wants to teach them. Paul's theology, especially the manifold beauty of the gospel, is of first importance (1 Corinthians 15:3). But before he teaches the gospel, he wants them to know that he loves them.

The main thing that Paul does to communicate love to his readers is that he tells them of a certain regular occurrence in his life. The occurrence is so regular that Paul hyperbolically describes it as occurring *"unceasingly"* (1:9). He remembers them in *prayer*. This habit of Paul's life is to his Roman friends a warm expression of love, but to us it is also a fleshed-out picture—a living example—of what a Christian does when he has arrived at the point of being fully enlivened by the gospel. Paul is our example of what it looks like to be alive in Christ. It is a life of daily, hourly, even minute-by-minute *prayer*.

Paul describes his own prayer habit as being *unceasing*, which explains why he later exhorts others to the same (1 Thessalonians 5:17). Paul kept his heart continually open to God. It is hard to describe what this constant prayerfulness is like, especially since I personally have only experienced it in seasons, and even now only return there in fits and starts. But I can at least testify that it is a real place where the Christian heart is able to abide. Even though I find it a struggle to stay there, it is the place where the heart is most at home. Paul shows us a glimpse of his own prayer life when he tells the Romans about how he prays for them. As Paul communed with God day in and day out, his mind repeatedly thought of the Roman Christians, and his spirit cried out for certain things on their behalf. What characterized these prayers that Paul offered?

Paul's prayers for these believers were first of all *celebratory*. He became joyful when he prayed for them. The Roman believers had noteworthy faith. Perhaps it was the endurance of their faith, remaining Christian in a hostile city where Christians were beginning to face persecution. Perhaps it was their boldness in preaching a message that most hearers were calling foolish. Whatever it was, stories of their faith had reached Paul, and one can almost picture him being gleeful about it.

To better understand Paul's joy, a bit of background as to how the Roman church was born is worth exploring. There were some from Rome who were visiting Jerusalem on the day the church itself was born (read Acts 2). These men and women saw the power of God when the Spirit fell. But they were only a few people returning to the capital of the greatest empire the world had ever seen. Romans were a people who valued power. They delighted in their conquering of the nations. They were proud to be Roman. But the greatest power rested upon those few believers, and these little children were beginning to walk in it. It is likely that from those few who caught the Spirit's flame in Jerusalem, a fledgling church formed in Rome, and their number began to grow. Before very long, their faith was "being proclaimed throughout the whole world" (1:8).

Paul kept thanking God with celebratory joy whenever he thought of the Roman believers. Then Paul's prayers would turn to *supplication*. One desire kept arising in his heart, giving rise to an oft-repeated request: "Dear God, let me go to Rome!" Paul must have prayed this for a long time, because at some point, "*now at last*" accompanied the answer that Paul sought. Why did he want to go so badly? If we can find in the text what motivated Paul's desire, then we will find for ourselves the kind of thing for which we should be praying.

First, he wanted to fan the flame that was already in them: "that I may impart some spiritual gift to you, that you may be established" (1:11). Seeing that the meeting of Paul's desire was not just over the horizon, I think this is what occasioned the writing of the book of Romans. He could not get to them physically, but he could get a letter to them. He could lay out the glorious truths of the gospel and thus establish them in the Truth.

I resonate with Paul's decision here. So often I have desired to preach the gospel when circumstances did not afford the opportunity. Few barriers, however, are able to withstand that which is put into writing. It was my prayers for Roman Catholics that stirred up my soul to write this commentary on the book of Romans. Paul's unceasing prayerful desire to see the Romans led to his decision to write to them. So, in part, we owe our possession of the book of Romans—a book that helped shape history—to Paul's prayer habit. How do we know what spiritual gift would be imparted to people we know if only we were consistent about praying for them? God often uses us to answer our prayers for others to be spiritually established.

Second, Paul wanted his own flame to be fanned. As passionate about Jesus Christ as Paul was, he wanted to be around other fire-baptized, gospel-preaching Jesus lovers who would inspire him and encourage him to burn even brighter. There are few things that encourage Christians to run faster, work harder, endure more, and enjoy Christ more than being in the same room as a man on fire for God. Paul wanted to get to the Roman Christians because he was always hungry for more of Christ. We need to pray for deep interaction with other believers, just as Paul prayed in order "that I may be encouraged together with you while among you, each of us by the other's faith, both yours and mine" (1:12).

Finally, Paul cared for the yet unbelieving citizens of Rome and the world. He knew the strategic importance of reaching Rome. He wanted to "obtain some fruit among you also, even as among the rest of the Gentiles" (1:13). By *obtaining fruit*, Paul meant *making disciples*. Rome was the capital of the world. All roads led to it and went out from it. If the gospel, which is news to be carried, were to be embraced there, where in the world would that lead? When we pray, do we ask God for ways to proactively and strategically advance the gospel to the nations? We must learn to pray for the "greater progress of the gospel" (Philippians 1:12).

Verses 1:8-13 are about prayer. All the saints, that's all of us who believe, need to learn how to *celebrate* and *supplicate* in prayer. Our supplications ought to be for the building up of other believers (Philippians 1:9-11), for our own edification and faithfulness in ministry (Romans 15:30-33), and for a door to be opened for the preaching of the word (Colossians 4:3).

The preacher of the gospel (every believer is like Paul in Romans 15:16 in being called to the priestly role of preaching the gospel) does not only have a ministry that comes into contact with unbelieving people. His or her ministry must first of all remain in contact with the Lord Jesus Christ. There in the place of prayer, offering *thanks* (1:8) and making *requests* (1:10), the minister serves God in the spirit (1:9). This inward work is not as dramatic as preaching from city to city. But without it, there will be no power in the outer work.

It was Paul's prayer for the Romans that inspired the writing of this profound book. Three years after its writing, God would grant Paul's request to go to Rome, but probably not in the way that Paul had in mind as he submitted to the "will of God" (1:9) to answer Paul's request however God saw fit. Acts chapters 21-28 tell the story of how God brought Paul through beatings, imprisonments, shipwreck and snake bite to get him to Rome. For Paul, Rome was the destination of his heart and Spain after that (Romans 15:24). For us, let us continue to follow the Romans Road to that destination of being completely given over, like a slave to his owner, to the Lord Jesus Christ, and so to know what it means to really live. Paul is our example of a man whose heart had come alive. What we see him doing outwardly is only an outworking of the inward life of prayer that Paul experienced between himself and the Lord Jesus Christ.

5

Lost

*"I am under obligation both to Greeks and to barbarians,
both to the wise and to the foolish"*

—Romans 1:14

So far in the overview (1:1-17), Paul gave us a picture of the *destination* we seek from the Romans Road. It is the place of becoming a slave (1:1a), but a slave belonging to the only One worthy of owning the life of another—Jesus Christ our Lord (1:4). This enslavement is paradoxically free (1:1b), showered in grace (1:5) and the fullest expression of what it means to really be alive (1:7). It is a heart on fire—motivated by a mission (1:8b), passionate in prayer (1:9), celebrating (1:8a), supplicating (1:10), loving (1:11) and being loved (1:12).

In order to get us to this destination, Paul overviewed several key points of the *gospel* (1:1.) The basis, or foundation, for the gospel is the Old Testament (1:2). The content of the gospel is centered upon Jesus (1:3). Jesus is a member of the Trinity (1:3-4). Jesus is fully human (1:3) and fully God (1:4). All glory belongs to Jesus, because everything we have is owed to His grace (1:5). Without these points on the map, any so-called gospel is a fraud. But upon that map of the gospel that is the book of Romans, we have yet to establish the *starting point*. It is introduced here in

1:14-15 and will be summarily proven in the first major section, spanning from 1:18-3:20.

The starting point that is often missed, even by those who may identify themselves with a "Christian" label, is the universal *lostness* of humankind. The gospel says that the problem of sin is far worse than human reasoning would ever assume. The book of Romans provides us with a mirror, held to our noses by the very hand of God, to show us what we are really like.

Perhaps one major reason many people do not accept the gospel is because they refuse to accept the starting point where the map of the gospel locates them. They are lost because they keep pushing the map away every time it shows them where they are and where they would remain if not for the appearance of a Savior.

The greatest danger that people face is not that they are lost so much as that they are too stubbornly prideful to admit it. Quick as they may be to admit that they make mistakes, they are painfully slow to conclude that they are hopelessly sinful.

They keep assuming that they have only stumbled and tumbled a short distance from the path that will take them home. "Given just a little while longer," they keep telling themselves, "I will find my way." They can admit that they are not perfect, but they do not know how far away from the path of righteousness they really are. They are without resources in the center of a million-square-mile jungle. Seeing only the canopy above and the trees in their view, they assume their home is but a stone's throw away. But in reality, home is unreachably far. Without a rescuer, they are lost forever. Without a Savior, they are dead already.

1:14-15   I am under obligation both to Greeks and to barbarians, both to the wise and to the foolish. So, for my part, I am eager to preach the gospel to you also who are in Rome.

In the section spanning from Romans 1:18-3:20, Paul will prove that wretches like us start out in a desperate and desolate place. We are in the same predicament as everyone else who descends from Adam and Eve. We may find some comfort when we see that we're not the only ones. But if being lost in sin, separated from the life of God forever, is what we all have in common, then our equality is a small comfort. If hell is hot and humans are still capable of having any sort of compassion there (Luke 16:28 indicates that we are), is there any relief afforded to us if we see loved ones suffering a similar eternal punishment as we are? Paul states in

Romans 9:3 that he would rather go to hell alone than for his kinsmen to have to go. Paul will lump us together in Romans 1:18-3:20, but it is not for the purpose of making us feel safe. There is no safety in numbers when faced with the wrath of God.

The point is that Paul is *"under obligation"* (1:14) to preach the gospel to *everyone*. Whether a person is the most sophisticated Greek or the most uncouth barbarian, no matter the language they speak, no matter how wise or foolish they may be, Paul must tell them the truth, whether or not they will ultimately accept it. Like a watchman on the tower is *obligated* to sound an alarm when an enemy is approaching, Paul is duty-bound. As a weatherman must not keep silent when his instruments detect a Category 5 Hurricane bearing down upon a coastal city, Paul is *under obligation* to not stay silent.

Paul is bound and determined to get to Rome because he accepts the weight of obligation. Paul is *under obligation* because the Romans are *under wrath*. Their condition is far worse than the sophisticated Roman mind would ever assume. They are hopelessly lost, destined to die, destined to perish in hell. Paul has the remedy. He is obligated to get to Rome and share it. The gospel is the remedy. Paul is duty-bound to travel the Appian Way, to pass the Three Inns, to go tell it on the seven mountains of Rome (Acts 28:15).

But were the people of Rome really that bad? Are people in general really that sinful that we deserve eternal punishment? Could God really be like an advancing army (Revelation 19:11-16)? Could God really be the One who allows natural disasters, what insurance policies have called "acts of God," for His own reasons (Job 1:12, Genesis 19:24, Revelation 8:5-13)? Is the human race really lost?

Most people, when they consider whether or not God can have wrath and bring judgment, picture themselves as innocent civilians in a city under siege. Far from being wicked members of an evil population, they see themselves as moral citizens of a good city. But if this is the case with us, then why do we see so much war in the world? We blame the bad guys and rightfully so. But are we really so much different? What are we capable of doing? What is in our hearts? Would we be the enemy carrying a sword against the hapless victims of an innocent city if it were not for the restraining power of God mercifully keeping our nature in check? Would we be the ones shooting, massacring and beheading those who disagree with us if we were not raised in a culture that bears the merciful marks of having been highly influenced and partially formed by the teachings of Jesus?

What makes us see ourselves as innocent when every form of evil can be found somewhere in our hearts, dormant though it may lay? What if it is only the merciful hand of God that stays the hurricane, the earthquake, the tornado, the volcano, the melting of polar ice, or the direct hit of a giant meteor? What if He lifts His merciful hand from time to time so that we would understand that *justice* alone would demand that His hand of *mercy* never be there at all? What if the way we see ourselves does not match the reality of who we really are?

Being *"under obligation"* (1:14) to preach the gospel to every living soul means that every living soul is under God's judgment. This is the hardest point of the gospel to accept. Many people who hear these things will turn against the messenger. They will secretly or overtly judge Paul to be a bigot. If they write him off as a product of his time, they will turn their ire against those of us who echo what he taught.

The truth is that God inspired what Paul taught about the spiritual lostness of the human race. Even if you or I choose not to accept where God places us on the map, we are no less in the million-mile jungle. Even if you or I choose not to believe that God has a right to judge and will exercise that right in the way that He has revealed, we still live in a world where disaster could strike in a moment, where death awaits us all as a matter of course, and where even parents cannot protect their children from this same inevitable fate.

These are the realities, so what other explanation will do? Should we accept the worldview of the evolutionary biologist? In our hearts, we know that the very presence of mass and energy in the Universe demands a Source. If we keep tracing back in our minds through the supposed stages of evolution and the Big Bang before that, we arrive back at where we already are—knowing that there must be a God. The original ball of mass and energy had to come from somewhere.

If there is a God who created all that is, then where is He now? If we are only an innocent city under siege and God refuses to prevent human suffering, then He must not be a loving God. Conversely, if He is just too distant to know about or change the events of our lives, then where did all His power go? The existence of a weak or unloving God is no more possible than the existence of this world without the existence of God. As hard as it is for any of us to accept, the only good explanation for the world as we know it is the one that Paul gives.

If you have found yourself stuck for a long time, perplexed by the suffering and death you see in the world, but unable to deny the patently obvious truth that the very presence of this world proves that there must be a God, then it is time for you to allow the book of Romans to locate you on the map. That the human race is spiritually lost is the only good explanation for the suffering and death we see in the world. Paul will prove the point in 1:18-3:20. But for now, to understand why Paul says he is "under obligation both to Greeks and to barbarians, both to the wise and to the foolish," (1:14) we must understand Paul's worldview that places all people together under sin and under judgment. If Paul met you, he would be "eager to preach the gospel to you also" (1:15). You and I are sinners, desperately wicked but mercifully allowed by God's common grace to live for however long He determines. You and I will rightfully die a physical and spiritual death unless God mercifully saves us.

6

Found

"For I am not ashamed of the gospel, for it is the power of God for salvation to everyone who believes, to the Jew first and also to the Greek"

—*Romans 1:16*

That the human race is spiritually lost is a tough pill to swallow. Coming to terms with this bad news is logically prerequisite to being able to appreciate the good news of salvation for what it is. But chronologically speaking, many of us never choke down the bitter pill until we are given a tall glass of living water (John 4:10). We end up accepting the bad and the good at the same time. It is true that all people are lost in sin, and our condition is so bad that we should even consider ourselves "dead" (Ephesians 2:1). But it also true that Jesus is "the resurrection and the life" (John 11:25). By the same power that He was resurrected from the dead, He is also able to give eternal life to our mortal bodies (Romans 8:11). As bad as the human condition is, there is sufficient power in the gospel to save us from sin and death. How the power of God to save people is discriminately manifested upon certain ones—namely those who believe—is the thesis statement of the book of Romans.

1:16-17   For I am not ashamed of the gospel, for it is the power
             of God for salvation to everyone who believes, to the
             Jew first and also to the Greek. For in it the
             righteousness of God is revealed from faith to faith; as
             it is written, "BUT THE RIGHTEOUS man SHALL
             LIVE BY FAITH"

Since Paul's worldview sees all people as being guilty of sin and under God's wrath, why would he be ashamed to proclaim the only way of escape for them? Paul sees the gospel as good news for all.

In our culture, people put on their best faces when out in public. We like to project ourselves as being good, moral, and decent people. We think that charity is assuming the best of others, accepting their facades, and tolerating anything that doesn't match up with our standards. Moreover, the word *tolerance* itself has been redefined to mean that we stop believing in moral standards. It is not enough to tolerate people, as in doing them no injustice. Now we have to affirm them and never say that sinful behaviors are what they are.

So, in such a culture of "tolerance", where there is no shame in sin so long as one keeps it sufficiently hidden, where it is instead considered shameful to call anything sin, how can we say that Jew and Greek alike are desperately lost in sin? Paul was not ashamed because his message didn't end with the bad news but continued on to the highest good. We can likewise find confidence and witness the gospel's power when we preach a complete message, not sugarcoating our sinful condition, but also not stopping there. Like Paul, we preach "*salvation*" (1:16).

The highest good is the righteousness of God. God's righteousness extends to the level of moral *perfection*. God's character is actually the standard of right and wrong. The good news reveals that moral perfection—absolute righteousness—is "*revealed from faith to faith.*" That is to say, God reveals His righteousness in people who have genuine faith. It's not that they behave perfectly. It's far from that. They sin like everyone else. But God credits His own righteousness to their account and looks at them as if they have never sinned.

On what condition does this take place? "*Everyone who believes*" (1:16) receives this tremendous gift. The "*righteousness of God*" (1:17) shows up in a person "*from*" the moment of "*faith*" and continues as he or she continues "*to*" have "*faith.*" "From faith to faith" (1:17) means that there is no other requirement. The imputation of righteousness removes the problem of sin, so the person becomes alive to God. The person who arrives at this destination—the point of genuinely believing in Jesus—has passed from death to life. They started out helplessly lost in sin, but found the way to "*salvation*" (1:16). Rescued from the death penalty that is owed to everyone who has sinned, the sinner is "*revealed*" to be sinless from that moment forward. He or she has become a saint. The person with the life of God inside is really alive.

Paul says, "the righteous man shall live by faith." He doesn't mean that a man's faithful moral living will catch God's eye and warrant His approval. Rather, the man is righteous because an alien righteousness—a righteousness that came from another place—was given to the man. It is "*the righteousness of God*" (1:17), not the righteousness of man. The man is alive because of it, although he contributed nothing to it. His only part was to have "faith," which is only trusting God for the promised gift of righteousness. The man is therefore not to be praised. Only God, who credits righteousness and makes the man alive, receives the glory for the transaction.

This is the thesis statement of the book of Romans, the tag line that opens eyes to the gospel. It has been changing lives since it was written, and still does so today. "*The righteous man shall live by faith.*" The gift of righteousness that says "*live*" to the dead sinner comes only "*by faith.*" Faith in the One the gospel concerns—the Son of God (1:3), fully human (1:3), fully God (1:4), Jesus Christ our Lord (1:4)—is the subject of the book of Romans. The seven major sections commend faith at every turn. "*Everyone who believes*" (1:16) will "*live*" (1:17) by the principles of the "*gospel*" (1:16).

SECTION 2

Nowhere Near Good Enough

Romans 1:18-3:20

7

Wrath

*"For the wrath of God is revealed from heaven against
all ungodliness and unrighteousness of men who
suppress the truth in unrighteousness"*

—Romans 1:18

The starting point of the gospel has been pinpointed on the map. It
locates every descendent of Adam and Eve, except the virgin-born
Son of God, in a helpless position, deeper in the jungle of sin than we ever
imagined. We are spiritually lost with no way of getting ourselves home. It
is even appropriate to say that we are spiritually dead.

> *"And you were dead in your trespasses and sins, in which you
> formerly walked according to the course of this world, according
> to the prince of the power of the air, of the spirit that is now
> working in the sons of disobedience. Among them we too all
> formerly lived in the lusts of our flesh, indulging the desires of the
> flesh and of the mind, and were by nature children of wrath, even
> as the rest" (Ephesians 2:1-3)*

Paul was "under obligation" (Romans 1:14) because all people
were under wrath. We were no longer living children of God, but were

instead dead "children of wrath." What can a spiritually dead child do for himself? Since he is "indulging the desires . . . of the mind," he doesn't want to accept what God says about his present condition. Even though he is nowhere near good enough for God, he thinks he is.

It is therefore merciful for God, speaking through Paul, to prove the charge in the hopes that further light will make hidden things visible (Ephesians 5:13) and remove the colored glasses through which we all tend to view ourselves. The map immediately located us, but now we need to take a more careful look at Romans 1:18-3:20 in order to come to terms with where it placed us. Our sinful hearts need convincing.

Romans 1:18-3:20 summarily destroys all human effort to justify self. If anyone is going to accept God's gift of salvation through Jesus Christ, then they first need to accept that they need saving. They must stop entertaining vain imaginations about how they look in the eyes of God and instead take a good hard look in the mirror of God's Word. Romans 1:18-3:20 is that merciful mirror of God that shows us what we are truly like.

1:18-23   For the wrath of God is revealed from heaven against all ungodliness and unrighteousness of men who suppress the truth in unrighteousness, because that which is known about God is evident within them; for God made it evident to them. For since the creation of the world His invisible attributes, His eternal power and divine nature have been clearly seen, being understood through what has been made, so that they are without excuse. For even though they knew God, they did not honor Him as God or give thanks, but they became futile in their speculations, and their foolish heart was darkened. Professing to be wise, they became fools, and exchanged the glory of the incorruptible God for an image in the form of corruptible man and of birds and four-footed animals and crawling creatures.

Romans 1:17 already told us the good news that God's righteousness "*is revealed*" to those who believe in Jesus Christ. That is to say, a gift is imputed to those who go "from faith to faith." God sends righteousness from heaven to earth, making alive those upon whom it falls and discriminating "by faith." Those who believe the gospel are spared. Those who do not believe are not spared. But spared from what? The good news proposition only makes sense if something else is already revealed from heaven, something from which everyone has need of being saved. The revelation of a gift from heaven is necessary because "the wrath of God *is revealed* from heaven." Bad news about God's wrath *is revealed* before good news about His mercy.

How is God's wrath revealed? We are not told of any outward manifestations that prove God is angry with humanity. That the world is filled with suffering and death is a clear indication that something is broken in the relationship between God and His creatures. But the text does not point to any hurricane, tornado, earthquake, or sign in the sky that would serve as an example of how the wrath of God *is revealed*.

Rather, the way in which God's wrath is revealed is by this very reminder here in Romans 1:18-23 and the words of every Christian who remembers this starting point when they share the gospel. God tells us what He knows about us, three things specifically. First, our thoughts, words and deeds are described as "*ungodliness.*" That is to say, what God would think, say, or do in many of our situations is very different from what we think, say, and do. The prefix "*un*" indicates that God sees the opposite of godliness in us.

Second, the same prefix "*un*" this time describes the extent to which we are righteous. Everything in heaven is righteous because heaven is the dwelling place of God. But God negates our vain imaginations and frustrates our desires to describe ourselves that way. We are unrighteous.

Finally, we compound our already grave condition when we "suppress the truth in unrighteousness." This *suppression* is the major subject of the paragraph. Whereas ungodliness and unrighteousness are simply given as descriptors from God's viewpoint with no examples given, when it comes to *suppression* of truth, the passage lays out how so. Like a blatant provocation after passing a tipping point, the grave offense Paul describes is sure to produce wrath. God is justifiably angry.

Already ungodly and unrighteous, people ought to fall down trembling and beg God for mercy. Instead, as Paul describes, they begin to entertain thoughts that God does not exist. They start to push what they know out of their mind and imagine a world where God's judgment doesn't matter. They invent gods of their own making, preferring to serve those gods in the way that they please. As cultures become more sophisticated, wooden figurines may give way to other things, like digital blips on screens (sports, shows, news, and social networking) or cars, houses, alcohol or relationships. But whatever we put in first place in our lives has become an idol. God has been replaced, exchanged for a god that serves the sinner, a god that doesn't judge sin and cares too little to experience wrath.

Without the gospel, people can go happily to their dying day. They will die in their sins and face the wrath of the true God. The starting point of the gospel, the gospel's first principle, shines a light on the true God in order that we would see Him before that Day of Judgment and see that we are not there in His presence. We need to see that He is not okay with us, as we stand. We need to remember what we once innately knew. There is one Divine Being who is eternally powerful.

I once visited CERN outside of Geneva, Switzerland. CERN is the leading research institution in the world when it comes to studying atomic particle collisions and how they shed light on what happened in the fractions of a second that preceded the supposed Big Bang. While there, I asked one of their scientists what theory prevails at CERN as to the origin of that ball of mass and energy that existed prior to the Big Bang. As it must always be, the CERN scientists are content to say that they do not know. They think they have the origins of the Universe traced out to within a fraction of a second, but they only have speculations as to where the ball of mass and energy came from in the first place. I was not surprised to hear this scientist say so. "For even though they knew God, they did not honor Him as God or give thanks, but they became futile in their speculations, and their foolish heart was darkened. Professing to be wise, they became fools".

This world's geniuses like Richard Dawkins and Stephen Hawking may float "brilliant" theories. They would have us believe that piggy-backing diamonds or alien seeding from another universe are plausible theories for the first appearance of life on the earth. But God inspired Paul to state the obvious.

Men chose to make idols because they preferred them to the implications of a Holy Creator God. They willfully convinced themselves to ignore God. "For since the creation of the world His invisible attributes, His eternal power and divine nature have been clearly seen, being understood through what has been made, so that they are without excuse." The presence of mass and energy obviously had to come from God. To deny this fundamental truth is not only to deny the obvious but also to deny what God has written on the human heart: "for God made it evident to them."

This is how the wrath of God *is revealed* from heaven. God wrote the knowledge of Himself on the human heart. But ungodly and unrighteous people deliberately suppress that knowledge, preferring instead to worship whatever they can make with their hands. When the gospel comes along and points out this reality, humanity's three-fold guilt is revealed for what it is. We are ungodly, unrighteous, and suppressing the truth. The message reveals the guilt.

Many people utterly despise hell-fire preachers because it is easier to hate a messenger than it is to consider their message. Some preachers may go too far, exhibit a superior judgmental attitude, or may even be themselves counterfeit preachers of the gospel. But being angry at those who preach about God's wrath does not negate the fact that God has wrath. Just as it requires God's special revelation in order for us to know that *God is love* (1 John 4:8), it requires His revelation in order for us to know that *He also has wrath* (Romans 1:18). But even now, as we consider Romans 1, the wrath of God *is revealed* against the ungodliness and unrighteousness of men who suppress the truth. We must not turn away too quickly from the mirror. Look now at the most obvious example that proves these things about us.

8

Impurity

*"Therefore God gave them over in the lusts of their
hearts to impurity, so that their bodies would be
dishonored among them"*

—*Romans 1:24*

Sexual impurity is the most obvious example of how ungodly and unrighteous we are. We demonstrate in our bodies that we suppress the truth in our minds. God stated his boundaries for sexual activity when He created the first man and the first woman (Genesis 2:21-25). Not only so, He wrote those boundaries on the human conscience. Sex was a gift from God to married people to bring them together in unity, to potentially bring forth children, and to enjoy. Within the boundaries of God's created order, sex should be like any other aspect of the human experience. We should honor God with our bodies, thus bringing glory to God, even as we find joy in so doing. But since we have become unrighteous and ungodly, since we suppress God's truth, our bodies are given over to sexual sin.

1:24-25   Therefore God gave them over in the lusts of their
               hearts to impurity, so that their bodies would be
               dishonored among them. For they exchanged the truth

of God for a lie, and worshiped and served the creature rather than the Creator, who is blessed forever. Amen.

People wanted idols instead of the glorious God. They preferred their own self-delusion to the plain truth that was evident to their hearts. They chose the creature over the Creator. So, God *gave them over* to what they wanted.

God could have done differently. He could have changed their minds by cutting out their hearts. In place of a heart that is able to desire and to love, He could have hardwired the human body to speak words of praise by rote. But this would require the death of human personality, the removal of *free will*, and the creation of robots who are not human at all.

It understandably made God angry, and it surely broke His heart, but He chose instead to let people go on suppressing their knowledge of Him and devoting their minds to that which is only a part of this created world. Their minds now fixed on created things, it would not be long before the pinnacle of God's creation—the human—would become the primary object of their worship. They began to worship the creature—the human body—rather than the One who made humankind.

Human sexuality was created for unity within a husband-wife relationship, for reproduction, and for enjoyment. Sex was perfect when the world was just as God created it. But after Adam and Eve sinned, the world was broken and human sexuality became broken as well. It became the prime example of our broken relationship with God. If our minds are truly turned over to idols rather than the true God, then the clearest demonstration of that reality will be what we do with our bodies.

All people are alike in that we cannot reach adulthood without being tainted by some sort of sexual sin. Even if someone never behaves outwardly on the thoughts that enter the human mind, Jesus taught that "everyone who looks at a woman with lust for her has already committed adultery with her in his heart" (Matthew 5:28). That our hearts are so prone to lust is evidence that God has given us over to impurity. When bodies come together outside of marriage, "their bodies [are] dishonored among them" (Romans 1:24). Marriage was God's created boundary line for all sexual activity.

"For this reason a man shall leave his father and mother, and be joined to his wife; and they shall become one flesh. And the man and his wife were both naked and were not ashamed" (Genesis 2:24-25)

There is likely not an adult alive today who has never felt any shame about their sexual lives. That is owed to the reality that our text reveals. God gave us over to the dishonoring of our bodies because our minds had exchanged the knowledge of Him for idols. Our misdeeds *in our bodies* are symptomatic of ungodliness, unrighteousness and suppression of the knowledge of God *in our minds*.

Being *given over* also means that the natural shame that should accompany the dishonoring of our bodies quickly fades away. Whereas shame accompanied our first sexual sins, it weakened over time. How great is the sexual sin of those who can dishonor their bodies with someone to whom they are not married and feel no shame? People differ in how much shame they are still capable of feeling (how sensitive their consciences are), but even as Romans 1:25 ends with "amen," we ought to agree that our bodies have been dishonored among us and this proves that our minds have exchanged the glory of the Creator for bodies that are only a part of His creation.

1:26-27   For this reason God gave them over to degrading passions; for their women exchanged the natural function for that which is unnatural, and in the same way also the men abandoned the natural function of the woman and burned in their desire toward one another, men with men committing indecent acts and receiving in their own persons the due penalty of their error.

Two themes are carried further along in this passage. First, we *exchanged* the truth for a lie. Second, God did not obliterate human free will but rather *gave them over* to their desires.

As Paul's indictment of humanity moves forward, he brings up those who practice homosexual behaviors as proof that God "*gave them over.*" While not all of humanity fits this profile, the point is not to single out a particular group of people. Rather, the point is quite the opposite and very offensive to those who think that they were born straight, therefore nothing could ever change that. The point is that any one of *us* is capable of becoming one of *them*. *We*, in Romans 1:19-25, were the ones given over to the idols of our minds. *We* demonstrated our misplaced devotion through the dishonoring of our bodies. So, how are *we* different from *them* in Romans 1:26-27? We are no better, but are just as capable as any other of making a terrible *exchange* and being *given over* to degrading passions, including homosexual behaviors.

Just as all people exchange God for idols, some people exchange marital sex, a gift of God's design (Genesis 2:24-15) for same-gender sex, a repudiation of "the natural function" (Romans 1:26-27). We are not told how the genes of a person who commits indecent acts with a person of their same gender differs from the original genetic code that God gave to Adam and Eve. That would not justify the exchange. We are not told how environmental factors, like being abused as a child or being the victim of bad parenting, may predispose someone to make this exchange. It still wouldn't justify the behavior. We are, however, told that men and women who make this exchange are abandoning God's natural design in favor of something indecent.

The point being made is that homosexual behaviors are clear examples that people *exchange* truth for lies and are *given over* to those lies. Far be it from God to force someone to be pure. Rather, when they obey the "lusts of their hearts to impurity" (1:24), God may *give them over* to even worse, more unnatural, sexual behaviors. If God designed sex for a man and woman in marriage, then men and women will turn God's design into something of their own making, quite the opposite of God's. After crossing God's boundary line (marriage), some will even distort God's complimentary male/female design (heterosexuality). We are all *given over* to make such *exchanges*, and some people will take it even this far. But what we have all done with our bodies (1:24-25) is the prime example of how our ungodly minds suppress the truth in unrighteousness, thus heaping up God's wrath in heaven until the Day of Judgment, which day we have convinced ourselves will never come.

9

Depraved

"And just as they did not see fit to acknowledge God any longer, God gave them over to a depraved mind, to do those things which are not proper"

—*Romans 1:28*

Sexual immorality was given as the prime example of the unrighteousness of humankind. The main idea was that even the human body—an instrument created for the worship of the Creator—has been turned into an instrument of idolatry. People worship the human body instead of the Maker. We ignore the truth, cross God's boundaries, and lose our sense of right and wrong. But sexual impurity is only the first of many examples that prove that our minds have become corrupted. The word Paul uses to describe our minds is *"depraved,"* meaning corrupted, wicked, defiant, or evil. Because *our minds* have exchanged the truth of God for a lie, our minds are given over to depravity, and our lives follow course, being given over to all sorts of sin.

1:28-32   And just as they did not see fit to acknowledge God any longer, God gave them over to a depraved mind, to do those things which are not proper, being filled with all unrighteousness, wickedness, greed, evil; full

> of envy, murder, strife, deceit, malice; they are
> gossips, slanderers, haters of God, insolent, arrogant,
> boastful, inventers of evil, disobedient to parents,
> without understanding, untrustworthy, unloving,
> unmerciful; and although they know the ordinance of
> God, that those who practice such things are worthy of
> death, they not only do the same, but also give hearty
> approval of those who practice them.

This is now the third time that the book of Romans says, "*God gave them over.*" Amazingly, even after hearing that "*they*" are the ones whose bodies are dishonored among them (1:24-27), even knowing his or her own sexual sins, the reader may take in this list and ask, "who are *they* that do these things?" Who are these terrible people that Paul is talking about? It is you and I, dear reader, it is us! When our text says *they* did not see fit to acknowledge God any longer, it is talking about you and me. We are those who prefer idols to the true God (1:18-23). We are the ones who suppress God in our minds and dishonor Him with our bodies (1:24-25). We are the ones that "God [gave over] to a depraved mind, to do those things which are not proper" (1:28).

Having already dealt with sexual sins (1:24-27), Paul gives us twenty-one other examples of how a depraved mind works itself out in real life. Since these descriptors characterize what each of us is really like, it is no wonder that much of Reality TV tends to be based upon people who practice these things. The twenty-one examples of depravity are unrighteousness, wickedness, greed, evil, envy, murder, strife, deceit, malice, gossip, slander, hatred of God, insolence, arrogance, boastfulness, invention of evil, disobedience to parents, lack of understanding, untrustworthiness, lack of love, and lack of mercy. We are capable of deriving entertainment from watching twenty-one sins play out before our eyes.

Read over the list and ask yourself on which charge God would be bound to find you "not guilty." Perhaps you say "murder" because you never killed anyone. But don't you see that it is the "depraved mind" that is the subject of the paragraph, from which comes the things that we do? If we harbor anger in our hearts, then we violate a deeper meaning of "murder." It is certainly not as bad as physically murdering someone, but it is enough to expose a depraved mind in the eyes of God who sees the heart. This is why Jesus said, "'You shall not commit murder' … but I say to you that everyone who is angry with his brother shall be guilty before the court" (Matthew 5:21-22). We have all murdered in our thoughts. Are there any examples on the list that do not expose something wrong in your own heart? Even if you say so, I will not believe you, because "deceit" is on the list, and the mirror does not lie.

Our text tells us that to be guilty of any one of these is to be "worthy of death" (1:28). Yet we are guilty of them all. And to compound the problem, our sins affect other people. Not only do we have victims of our greed, gossip, or unloving behavior, but we encourage others to be like us. When a daughter sees her mother in a fit of rage, that dear girl learns to act like her mom. When a son hears his father tell a lie, he learns a new tactic for getting what he wants. We lead others into sin by the example we set. Not only so, we sometimes even advocate for the very things that lead people to death. When we tell others about a favorite television show that celebrates the twenty-one items on our above list of examples, we commend these things to others. Many people even take up political causes that "give hearty approval of those who practice" the very things that the mirror of God's Word reveals to be ungodly and unrighteous. We who are guilty and also lead others on a path to their own death are doubly "worthy of death" (1:28).

2:1-3   Therefore you have no excuse, everyone of you who passes judgment, for in that which you judge another, you condemn yourself; for you who judge practice the same things. And we know that the judgment of God rightly falls upon those who practice such things. But do you suppose this, O man, when you pass judgment on those who practice such things and do the same yourself, that you will escape the judgment of God?

Paul delivers the knockout punch. To the reader who is still holding to his integrity, Paul poses a question. Will you really escape God's judgment? You can see things like strife, deceit, slander and arrogance in others, but can you not see that God will rightly judge *you* for these very same things?

After all that has been exposed so far, from sexual sin to twenty-one other examples of the outworking of a depraved mind, who could still be standing? Surely, after listening to Paul, no one could think that they are godly, righteous, lovers of truth. But Paul knows yet one more thing about the depraved mind. When sin is being condemned, the depraved mind is quick to imagine the sin of others and slow to admit its own.

When Paul mentions greed, the depraved mind thinks of Wall Street bankers, even as it covets what they have. When Paul mentions lust, the depraved mind thanks God that he is not like those homosexuals, polygamists or promiscuous fornicators, even as it forgets or excuses its own past deeds. Here in this knockout punch (2:1-3), Paul exposes the sin of judgmentalism, whereby the sinner shifts the scales of judgment to favor oneself over and against another.

The hit lays us all out side by side. If anyone would attempt to approach God's bar to plead his case, he would have to trample upon everyone else. It is easy to despise a murderer, but what about the hater who is condemned by the same law? If we acknowledge that the hatefulness of another is wrong, then what does that say about the times we have hated someone who offended us? It is easy to find fault in everyone else when we hold up Romans 1 next to them. But Romans 2:1-3 turns the mirror back upon the man who holds it. It forces me to see myself. It exposes me and asks me how on earth I could ever escape the judgment of God.

10

Impartial

"For there is no partiality with God"

—Romans 2:11

The charges that Paul presses against us have been truly devastating. Paul began with a blanket summary that characterized us as unrighteous ungodly suppressors of truth. He began to prosecute the case by calling our sexual sins to the witness stand. He demonstrated from those sins that we exchange the glory of God for idols. Then he paraded twenty-one additional witnesses before the Judge, and each one confirmed the same thing about us. Then, inflicting another terrible wound, his prosecution exposed the ugly hypocrisy in us that allows us to judge other people.

After all this, we are as good as dead when Paul allows a glimmer of hope to peak through the shutters of the courtroom. It is the light of the gospel that Paul will take up preaching in the twenty-first verse of the third chapter. Hope rises here in the middle of Paul's prosecution when we are reminded of the "richness of [God's] kindness and tolerance and patience." We ought to realize at this point that God's kind tolerant patient mercy is our only hope of escaping judgment. But it is not yet time to fully reveal how anyone will escape judgment. We must wait for Romans 3:21 before we are shown that. It must first be established that although God will bring certain people to repentance, and He will forgive those who genuinely repent, no one will escape judgment by any other means than that. No one will escape without repentance and faith, because God is an impartial judge. We need to see the impartiality of the Judge.

2:4-11   Or do you think lightly of the richness of His kindness and tolerance and patience, not knowing that the kindness of God leads you to repentance? But because of your stubbornness and unrepentant heart you are storing up wrath for yourself in the day of wrath and revelation of the righteous judgment of God, who will render to each person according to his deeds: to those who by perseverance in doing good seek for glory and honor and immortality, eternal life; but to those who are selfishly ambitious and do not obey the truth, but obey unrighteousness, wrath and indignation. There will be tribulation and distress for every soul of man who does evil, of the Jew first and also of the Greek, but glory and honor and peace to everyone who does good, to the Jew first and also to the Greek. For there is no partiality with God.

Now the question becomes how individuals will respond to Paul's message, which is ultimately good news. After yoking all people together under sin (1:18-32) and giving no comfort for the moralist who judges himself better than others (2:1-3), Paul now reminds his readers that it isn't only God's wrath that *is revealed* from heaven. The righteousness of God *is revealed* from heaven to be a gift for the sinner. Understanding God's wrath was a necessary basis for understanding the good news Paul introduced in the overview (Romans 1:1-17). The gospel, underscored by the bad news about sin, must not be taken lightly. In the gospel, "the richness of [God's] kindness and tolerance and patience" (2:4) is extended to all. But not understanding their need, some take it lightly. Others do not. They humbly receive the gift with gratitude as they turn away from sin and receive forgiveness.

Paul's original audience was made up primarily of those who had come to repentance and placed their faith in Jesus Christ. Paul was, after all, writing to the church in Rome. He does not want them to be haughty. Instead they ought to be humble and always remember that it was only God's kindness that brought them to Jesus in the first place. The result of having genuinely believed the message of God's kindness is a life of "perseverance in doing good." The person who has tasted eternal life will strive to live a godly life in preparation for glory and honor and immortality.

On the other hand, those who take the bad news about sin and the good news about Jesus too lightly are exhibiting "stubbornness and [an] unrepentant heart" (2:5a). They may judge themselves to be okay, but Paul issues them this warning: "You are storing up wrath for yourself in the day of wrath and revelation of the righteous judgment of God" (2:5b). On what basis will they be condemned? First, the sins of Romans 1:18-2:3, which come from a depraved mind that suppresses God's truth, are summarized as being "selfishly ambitious" (2:8). This is the first charge, and it is enough to warrant God's wrath.

Secondly, they "do not obey the truth" (2:8). When confronted with their sin (1:18-2:3), when offered salvation in Jesus Christ (2:4), they do not repent and meet that message with faith (2:5). So, God calls their deeds "evil" (2:9) and promises them "wrath and indignation" (2:8). The penalty is justly deserved on account of having a sinful mind, body, and spirit *and then* rejecting God's kind offer of mercy through Jesus Christ.

It doesn't matter who you are. These are God's terms and conditions. He has said that He will not show partiality. Regardless of race or any outward thing that man looks upon, God looks at the heart. If He finds repentance there, together with faith in Jesus Christ, then He will give life. If He finds stubbornness, together with an ambivalent approach to the gospel, then He will give wrath and indignation.

2:12-16   For all who have sinned without the Law will also perish without the Law, and all who have sinned under the Law will be judged by the Law; for it is not the hearers of the Law who are just before God, but the doers of the Law will be justified. For when Gentiles who do not have the Law do instinctively the things of the Law, these, not having the Law, are a Law to themselves, in that they show the work of the Law written in their hearts, their conscience bearing witness and their thoughts alternately accusing or else defending them, on the day when, according to my gospel, God will judge the secrets of men through Christ Jesus.

Since God chose Abraham from among all the people of earth and from his seed raised up a chosen people that He calls the "apple of His eye" (Zechariah 2:8), it might appear that God shows partiality. But here Paul instructs us as to how it is that God deals impartially with individuals, even though He created a nation of particular people to carry out certain of His purposes.

It wasn't only Israel to whom God gave the moral law. The Jews were blessed to have the Ten Commandments written on stone (Exodus 20), but even without them, Jew and Gentile alike have the law of God written upon our hearts. Why is it that we find marriage in virtually every culture on earth, regardless of whether or not the people know Genesis 2:24-25? Why is it that all cultures have laws against stealing or murder? It is because God wrote His moral law on the hearts of men.

But like the tablets upon which God gave the Ten Commandments to Israel, the hearts upon which God writes are made of stone. Just because people sometimes instinctively do what is right does not mean that they are good, moral people. It means that they have a conscience to govern them. But the point is that while we all have a conscience, all of us still sin and will perish before the Judgment Seat of God. We have God's law written upon our hearts, but we are so stubborn, our hearts are so hard, that we do the very things that we know to be wrong at the core of our being. The secrets of our hearts will be laid out next to the law that is written on our hearts (Romans 2:16). "All who have sinned . . . will also perish" (Romans 2:12).

2:17-24   But if you bear the name "Jew" and rely upon the Law and boast in God, and know His will and approve the things that are essential, being instructed out of the Law, and are confident that you yourself are a guide to the blind, a light to those who are in darkness, a corrector of the foolish, a teacher of the immature, having in the Law the embodiment of knowledge and of truth, you, therefore, who teach another, do you not teach yourself? You who preach that one shall not steal, do you steal? You who say that one should not commit adultery, do you commit adultery? You who abhor idols, do you rob temples? You who boast in the Law, through your breaking the Law, do you dishonor God? For "the name of God is blasphemed among the Gentiles because of you," just as it is written.

Religious people are often the first to object when told that they are sinners who are destined to perish. They assume that because they believe in the law and even teach it to others, they will be excused for breaking it.

Paul is addressing Jews in this passage, but similar questions could be posed to followers of other religions as well. Muslims have their five pillars, their Qur'an and their Sunnah, but believe and teach it as much as they will, are there any laws of God the Muslim has broken? Even if someone accepts the moral codes of Islam or the Eight-fold path of Buddhism instead of the Ten Commandments of Judaism, are they not guilty of law-breaking at some moral point? God's standard is truly written in the Law He gave through Moses, but since the Law is also written on human hearts, moral governance appears everywhere in the world. But the teachers of these codes are themselves law-breakers just like the rest of us.

2:25-29   For indeed circumcision is of value if you practice the Law; but if you are a transgressor of the Law, your circumcision has become uncircumcision. So if the uncircumcised man keeps the requirements of the Law, will not his uncircumcision be regarded as circumcision? And he who is physically uncircumcised, if he keeps the Law, will he not judge you who though having the letter of the Law and circumcision are a transgressor of the Law? For he is not a Jew who is one outwardly, nor is circumcision that which is outward in the flesh. But he is a Jew who is one inwardly; and circumcision is that which is of the heart, by the Spirit, not by the letter; and his praise is not from men, but from God.

There is no chance of earning God's approval by keeping the outward observances prescribed by religious teachers. Jewish individuals thought that by being born Jewish, they were included in the covenant by the symbol of circumcision and thus right with God. But this was never the case.

The requirement of the Law was obedience, at which point everybody stumbled. But the Law also included a provision for sin. If sinners humbly brought their sacrifices to the altar for the Levites to offer up, the sinner found forgiveness. God would look upon the hearts of every individual Jew, and where He found the obedience of faith, a certain trust in God's provision for sin, He circumcised their heart. That is to say, God included among His eternal family only those who truly repented of sin and believed in Him for the forgiveness of sin.

Once Jesus died for sins and rose again, the outward covenant symbol of circumcision was no longer needed. God would continue to keep His promises to the nation of Israel, but every individual on the planet was invited to be in a new covenant with God. Whether Jew or Gentile, slave or free, male or female, all were offered the same Holy Spirit, who would enter into the human heart and make that person a child of God. This "circumcision of the heart" would truly change the person. It would turn a heart of stone into a heart of flesh. A person's seared conscience would become lively again. Desires would change. Satisfaction would now be found in the things of God rather than the things of man.

What people really need is not outward religious observances but a change of heart that only comes "by the Spirit" (2:29). Becoming a Christian is therefore not a show to impress others, but a change of heart that God sees, in which He takes pleasure.

11

Misunderstanding

"What then? Are we better than they? Not at all; for we have already charged that both Jews and Greeks are all under sin"

—Romans 3:9

The impartiality of God, such that even Jews—the "children of God" (Deuteronomy 14:1)—will not escape God's wrath unless they repent and believe in Jesus, was bound to be misunderstood. Paul, who was himself a Jew, anticipated that some would wrongly conclude that Paul saw no special place for Israel in the plan of God. He also remembered that people had often misunderstood the gospel of grace that he preached, mistaking it for lawlessness that grants people a license to sin. So, at this point in the book, Paul suspends the development of his argument to answer some of the objections that he knows will arise in the minds of some of his readers.

3:1-8   Then what advantage has the Jew? Or what is the benefit of circumcision? Great in every respect. First of all, that they were entrusted with the oracles of God. What then? If some did not believe, their unbelief will not nullify the faithfulness of God, will it? May it never be! Rather, let God be true though every man be found a liar, as it is written, "that you may be justified in your words, and prevail when you are judged." But if our unrighteousness demonstrates the righteousness of God, what shall we say? The God who inflicts wrath is not unrighteous, is He? (I am speaking in human terms.) May it never be! For otherwise, how will God judge the world? But if through my lie the truth of God abounded to His glory, why am I also still being judged as a sinner? And why not say (as we are slanderously reported and as some claim that we say), "Let us do evil that good may come"? Their condemnation is just.

Paul now puts to rest some misunderstandings. What Paul actually faces here are more like criticisms, even deliberate obfuscations of what Paul preached in his gospel. Two charges are levied against Paul and his message.

First, there were those who thought that Paul was speaking like a Gentile at best or an anti-Semite at worst. Paul himself was "circumcised the eighth day, of the nation of Israel, of the tribe of Benjamin, a Hebrew of Hebrews" (Philippians 3:5). But although Paul was Jewish through and through, he did not believe that this made him right with God. In order to be right with God, he had to repent of sin and turn to Jesus Christ, just like everyone else. And since *everyone else* was therefore on the same footing, many Jews thought that Paul was denying the unique place that Israel holds as the apple of God's eye.

Paul gives one example to dispel this criticism. The Jews "were entrusted with the oracles of God" (3:2). This one thing is what mattered most in making Israel special. The Word of God didn't come through Plato, Socrates, Aristotle, or Buddha. God chose Abraham, Moses, David, and all the Hebrew prophets to deliver His holy words to humanity. Their message was supremely focused on one descendant of Abraham, one prophet like Moses, one Son of David and Son of God, Jesus Christ our Lord. To have the writings that reveal the Christ is the greatest advantage that anyone could ever have, because eternal life comes through knowing Him.

There were then, as there are today, Jews who refused to believe in their Jewish Messiah. That reality in no way undercuts the "oracles of God." His Word is true, and Jews are blessed to have it, regardless of who among them are willing to believe.

Second, there were those who accused Paul of teaching lawlessness. One can frequently hear the same charge levied against Christians today. Since we, like Paul, say that obeying the law can never accrue enough credit to our account to make us acceptable to God, our accusers say that we advocate throwing caution to the wind. Our teaching, according to them, allows people to run out and sin as heartily as they desire. Provided they simply repent later and keep believing in Jesus, Christians are supposedly forgiven anyway. So, there is no reason to obey any of God's laws. This is a human argument that Paul faced, and he reacts to it as strongly as he reacted to the charge of being anti-Jewish. "May it never be!"

Paul negates the assertion. The impartation of the Holy Spirit, who circumcises the heart of the one who receives Him, is sure to produce righteousness in that one. If someone claims to be a Christian and yet lives a haphazard life of deliberate lawbreaking, then such a one hasn't received Paul's teaching at all. A person doesn't give God glory by providing Him with sin to forgive. God forgives because God is merciful. But the power of the gospel is demonstrated to the world when God gives power to those whom He has forgiven to live righteously. When Christians fail to do so, our unfaithfulness does not negate God's faithfulness to His gospel, but neither does it bring glory to Him. God is glorified in us when we remain satisfied in Him and keep His laws because that is what our transformed hearts desire to do.

A misunderstanding can also arise from the opposite direction. As people contemplate the Christian message, they look at Christians as representatives of the Christ that we claim to follow. Paul adequately addressed the charge that Christians are free to live loose immoral lives, but the opposite charge is sure to follow. Someone will say that we think we are better than everyone else. Because we condemn as sin everything that the Bible calls sins, some people will regard Christians as being judgmental. To whatever degree we overcome sin in our own lives by the power of the gospel; our accusers will say that we think we ourselves better than others.

3:9-20   What then? Are we better than they? Not at all; for we have already charged that both Jews and Greek are all under sin; as it is written, "There is none righteous, not even one; There is none who understands, There is none who seeks for God; All have turned aside, together they have become useless; There is none who does good, There is not even one. Their throat is an open grave, with their tongues they keep deceiving, the poison of asps is under their lips, whose mouth is full of cursing and bitterness, their feet are swift to shed blood, destruction and misery are in their paths, and the path of peace they have not known. There is no fear of God before their eyes." Now we know that whatever the Law says, it speaks to those who are under the Law, so that every mouth may be closed and all the world may become accountable to God, because by the works of the Law no flesh will be justified in His sight; for through the Law comes the knowledge of sin.

We are alike in being nowhere near good enough. God's mirror doesn't lie. The book of Romans makes three big-picture charges against us. We are charged with ungodliness, unrighteousness, and suppression of truth (1:18-23). That our minds exchange God for idols is evidenced by what we do with our bodies. Sexual immorality shows that we worship the creature instead of the Creator, whose boundaries for sex we deliberately overstep (1:24-27). On top of that, we are shown twenty-one other ways that our depraved mind works itself out in our everyday lives (1:28-32). What's more, if someone imagines himself to be the exception, not as guilty of these things as the rest of us, then he only adds judgmentalism to the list of his transgressions (2:1-3).

Since God is impartial, without the gospel, no one will escape God's wrath (2:4-11). Having never read the Ten Commandments is no excuse, because the Law is written on the heart (2:12-16). The Jew is condemned by the Law of Moses (2:17-29), but that doesn't mean that there is no advantage to being a Jew (3:1-4). Nor does it mean that the gospel advocates lawlessness (3:5-8). Rather, God gave us the Law as a mirror to show us what we are really like (3:9-20).

The final description of what we are like (3:9-20) is the farthest thing from flattering. Our behavior is condemned as *unrighteous*. Our minds are so depraved that we may even consider ourselves religious when, in fact, "there is none who seek for God." And then there are the words that come out of our mouths. The mirror gives us a terrible image. "Their throat is an open grave." We are condemned for our lies and vicious words. Our speech is "full of cursing and bitterness." We are shown our violent ways, that which hurts other people. And then we are given the summary statement, the deathblow as it were, the charge that fully explains the description of us being "dead in our trespasses and sins" (Ephesians 2:1). The mirror shows it to us this way:

"There is no fear of God before their eyes" (Romans 3:18).

After fifty-two verses giving a theological understanding of the way we are (1:18-3:8), and after we've heard a stark description of the ugliness of our behaviors, thoughts, and words (3:9-17), our problem can really be summed up in this one sentence. We are only created beings, but the bottom line is, *we do not fear our Creator.* We live for ourselves, not for the One who made us, to whom we belong.

This being the case, what is God's point in telling us so? Mercy, dear reader. It is His mercy that tells us the truth before it is too late! Justice demands God's wrath directed at our unrighteousness. If He continues to *give us over* to do the things we ought not do, then the wrath we store up for ourselves will be just too much. On that Day of Judgment, when God rights every injustice, when every sin is punished, our punishment will be far too much to bear. He is a loving God as much as He is a just One, so He has made a way for us to be forgiven. More than that, He has made a way for us to be changed. But we cannot travel the road of repentance and faith until we accept our current location on the map.

The second section of Romans (1:18-3:20) has served us in this way. It has located us on the map. He did not hold up the mirror in order to condemn us. He showed us His righteousness, expressed in His Law, because "through the Law comes the knowledge of sin." Has Romans 1:18-3:20 accomplished this work in you? Are you willing to accept where the map locates you? Are you willing to agree that you are an ungodly, unrighteous sinner who suppresses your innate knowledge of God in favor of your idols? Will you admit that there is no fear of God before your eyes? If so, then you stand at the starting point, even on the brink of receiving the gift of eternal life. You would be condemned to hell if the Romans Road ended here. But thanks to God, it does not.

SECTION 3

Declared "Good" through Faith
Romans 3:21-5:21

12

Justified

"But now apart from the Law the righteousness of God has been manifested, being witnessed by the Law and the Prophets"

—*Romans 3:21*

The next thing that every sinner needs to see only makes sense to those who have seen the previous. But if one accepts the bad news about being helplessly lost, desperately sinful, and storing up wrath for the Day of Judgment, then the first two words of the third section of the book of Romans will be the most wonderful news the sinner has ever heard.

"But now"

With these words, the bad news about *us* gives way to *"the gospel of God"* (Romans 1:1), the thesis of the book of Romans. The gospel is good news about what God has done to save sinners like us. The Greek word νυνί, transliterated "nuni," meaning "but now," is an emphatic. It is a very strong way of saying "now," indicating a drastic change in the way things are going forward compared to how they were up until that point.

The great thing that every sinner needs to see is how a sinner can be saved. How does God grant salvation to sinners? On what condition is salvation given? When the apostle Paul brought the gospel to Europe for the first time, it didn't take long for him to get arrested for proclaiming the way of salvation (Acts 16). God didn't want the message kept in chains, bound with Paul in a prison, so He sent an earthquake that set the prisoners free. Seeing this extreme manifestation of God's power, the jailor asked Paul the ultimate question. "What must I do to be saved?" (Acts 16:30).

On what condition will a holy God be willing to declare that a sinner is "good?" How can I be good enough for God? Paul's answer was as simple as it was profound, "Believe in the Lord Jesus" (Acts 16:31). Hearing these words, the jailor saw a manifestation of God's righteousness. What he saw saved him. Seeing the earthquake didn't do it. Seeing the gospel saved the jailor. Romans 3:21-5:21 can likewise open our eyes to the truth.

> 3:21-22   But now apart from the Law the righteousness of God has been manifested, being witnessed by the Law and the Prophets, even the righteousness of God through faith in Jesus Christ for all those who believe; for there is no distinction

The great mystery of the gospel, which is even in this moment revealed, is that God does not judge people based upon the extent to which a person keeps God's moral laws, but rather upon whether or not a person trusts in Jesus. God's absolute righteousness—His complete moral perfection—is imputed to a person at the very moment he or she places faith in Jesus Christ. To stand innocently before God is therefore possible, not in the sense of having kept the Law perfectly, but as one who has received the gift of God's righteousness.

God is willing to look at "all those who believe" in Jesus Christ and count them as righteous. God looks at these certain people, as human as everyone else, and sees His own righteousness manifesting all over them. Like a cloud that has covered them, God sees only this, not the sin of the one encompassed. And this is not cloudy judgment, because the righteousness that God sees is not only a cloud covering, it is a miraculous overtaking by which the believing person is actually changed. In that "but now" (νυνί) moment, when the eyes of the sinner are opened and genuine trust in Jesus Christ takes over the sinner's soul, God's righteousness manifests in the sinner.

There is "*no distinction*." This gift is available to Jew and Gentile, slave and free, male and female. There is no condition attached to this gift except that it be received. This trust that one has in receiving the gift of salvation is described as "faith in Jesus Christ." The people who trust God for salvation are called "those who believe." Salvation is a free gift offered to all, a gift that needs to be accepted.

Even as this "gospel of God" (1:1) was first introduced in the overview as being "promised beforehand through His prophets in the holy Scriptures" (1:2), we are here reminded that the gospel is "witnessed by the Law and the Prophets" (3:21). It is not as if the Law is just thrown away when it is revealed that imputed righteousness comes to people apart from their own merits (apart from obeying the Law). Rather it is the Law that exposed our desperate need for salvation. And it is the Law that contains profound promises of a coming Messiah, even a Savior who would die and rise again. So, on the basis of the Law, all people are called to believe in Jesus, in order that the righteousness of God would manifest miraculously in them.

3:23-25a   For all have sinned and fall short of the glory of God, being justified as a gift by His grace through the redemption which is in Christ Jesus; whom God displayed publicly as a propitiation in His blood through faith.

It is hard to fully appreciate the good news of Romans 3:23-25a without having read what the book of Romans has said up to this point. It was essentially bad news that "all have sinned and fall short of the glory of God." But to "fall short" is a bigger deal than one might think. It means that we are ungodly and unrighteous. We suppress the truth in unrighteousness, preferring to worship the idols we make for ourselves rather than the true God. We are therefore given over to sin, to every kind of wickedness. We gossip, lie, curse, hate, and envy what others have. Our body is defiled by sexual sin. Our mind is corrupted. Our thoughts are ungodly. Our attitude is prideful. And then there are our words. Oh, how terrible are the things that have come out of our mouths. It shows that there is something wrong with our hearts.

The bottom line is that "there is no fear of God before [our] eyes" (Romans 3:18). This is the condition in which we will die. Without a Savior, we will surely go to hell, because the silence we hear from heaven is only a sign that we are storing up wrath in heaven for the Day of Judgment. The bad news is that God's wrath is revealed from heaven in His silence toward our sin, which is proof that we are given over to sin and destined for wrath on Judgment Day.

"But now" (Romans 3:21) the good news is that God **justifies through faith**. To "justify" (δικαιόω , or dikaioo, in the Greek) means to declare righteous. It is a judicial term. When God, the Judge of all, sits on His throne on the day in which He will judge the world, He will declare of each person in whom was found faith in Jesus Christ that he or she is righteous. This simple message is the gospel.

Like a radiant diamond that shines forth manifold complexity from within, so the simple gospel has deep and intrinsic beauty that unveils itself as the beholder moves around it and examines it from different angles. Our current text separates the word "justified" from "through faith." In the middle, we find seven prepositional phrases that capture different beams of light that shine forth from the gospel. Each phrase is intrinsic to the gospel, meaning that it is part and parcel of the message that must be received "through faith." Believers may not understand all the theological terms, but their meaning must be included in what the believer has come to trust. The believer must see the light.

The **first** essential phrase that illuminates the meaning of the gospel is "*as a gift.*" It is crucial to understand that we did nothing to earn the miraculous manifestation of God's righteousness. Nor can our good works even begin to pay God back. People are declared righteous because God *gives* His righteousness. It is not something that people earn in any way.

Which brings us to the **second** phrase. The gift comes "by His grace," meaning out of the goodness of His heart. God leans in toward a person to bless them with kindness simply because God has a kind heart. So the combined phrases "*as a gift by His grace*" mean that whereas people bring nothing to the table, God's essential goodness bestows a free blessing upon them.

The **third** prepositional phrase is "through the redemption." Redemption (ἀπολύτρωσις , apolutrosis) is a transactional term where something or someone is released when a payment is received, as in the payment of a ransom. If a slave was taken out of the possession of an owner and the owner finds a way to buy him or her back, he has redeemed his slave. In the same way, all people once belonged to our Maker, but when God gave us over to our own depraved minds, we actually became slaves of sin. But now (here is the gospel), God redeemed His slave. Not leaving the slave there in bondage to sin, God bought us back and gave us the freedom of being a slave ("doulos" in Romans 1:1) to the One to whom it is fitting that we would belong.

Fourth, the gospel tells us *which* redemption accomplished our freedom. It is a very distinct redemption. It was the redemption "which is in Christ Jesus." Only the Christ, the Jewish Messiah, could accomplish so great a salvation.

Fifth, even as slaves were often sold publicly in an open market, God "displayed [the Messiah] publicly." He was exposed on a hill overlooking Jerusalem, even hoisted up above the earth for all to see.

Sixth, this public display of the Messiah was done "as a propitiation." Propitiation (ἱλαστήριον, hilasterion) is an offering that appeases the wrath of God. We have already seen that the wrath of God is revealed from heaven by the deafening silence of a Deity who gives people over to their idols (1:18), because what God allows in the present time is only an indication that people are storing up wrath for a future Day of Judgment. "But now" (3:21) the silence is broken. A public display is made. A life is offered up as a sacrifice. The wrath of God is appeased.

Seventh and finally, the propitiation is "in His blood." Blood symbolizes the life of an offering. The Old Testament established this symbolism. "For the life of the flesh is in the blood, and I have given it to you on the altar to make atonement for your souls; for it is the blood by reason of the life that makes atonement" (Leviticus 17:11). Sacrifices were *really* bloody, because in the gruesome giving of life, God's wrath is graphically demonstrated, and the one who is spared becomes truly aware of what he or she was spared. Wrath is poured out on a sacrifice in place of a guilty party. The offering is a substitute that bears the wrath of God instead of the one who deserves it. The blood of Jesus, therefore, was the price that God paid in order to redeem sinners from the slave market of sin.

When we are taught that God "*justifies . . . through faith,*" we must not approach such news casually or take it for granted. We must gaze carefully at the manifold beauty of this radiant diamond that is the gospel. Here is a *gift* for which we pay nothing. Here is *grace* when we have earned wrath. Here is *redemption* when our cruel taskmaster was inescapable. Here is the *Christ* when the hope of Israel had waned for so long. Here is a *public display* that the world must never forget having seen. Here is *propitiation* when the wrath we had accrued for ourselves was overwhelming. Here is the *blood* of that innocent Lamb hanging upon a tree. Here is our righteousness. Here is our salvation. Here is our only hope. Here is life. It is here in the gospel for all who believe. Justification by faith is not a dead religious doctrine. It is ineffable. It is what every sinner most desperately needs to see. It is more than good enough. It is glorious.

13

Glory

"Where then is boasting? It is excluded. By what kind of law? Of works? No, but by a law of faith"

—*Romans 3:27*

Being justified by faith means that God passes over sins. He does not punish a genuine believer for his or her sins. Unbelievers must still face punishment, but the sins of believers are completely passed over. The seven prepositional phrases that interject between the words *"justified"* and *"through faith"* in Romans 3:23-25a underscore the meaning of justification by faith. But is justice really served when God judges the world this way, rather than judging every person according to His or her own merits?

The concept of justice is not a higher power than God Himself. It is not something to which God is bound, because if that were the case, then Almighty God would not be the highest power in the Universe. He would be subject to another. But God, not Lady Justice, is the Glory over all creation.

Justice is only an attribute of God. God *is just* in the same way that God *is love*. His person and character actually define the meaning of the terms "justice" and "love." So, the way in which He has chosen to judge the world He created is most certainly just, and in His kindness, He has chosen to demonstrate how His own demands for justice have been satisfied. The demonstration of God's justice brings glory to God.

3:25b-26   This was to demonstrate His righteousness, because in the forbearance of God He passed over the sins previously committed; for the demonstration, I say, of His righteousness at the present time, so that He would be just and the justifier of the one who has faith in Jesus.

The gospel is a revelation of the righteousness of God. The thesis statement of the book of Romans is the gospel. In the gospel, "the righteousness of God is revealed from faith to faith; as it is written, 'But the righteous man shall live by faith'" (Romans 1:17). The "one who has faith in Jesus" (3:26) is declared righteous.

This declaration of righteousness is only available to us because of the demonstration of Jesus Christ's righteousness that took place at a certain place and time. There on a hill called Calvary outside the gates of Jerusalem on the Day of the Passover, perhaps April 3rd, 33 AD, the ordinary course of this world was suspended. When Jesus was lifted up as a propitiation, God "demonstrated His righteousness." He showed the world that He has wrath, that there is nothing in His character whatsoever that will ever tolerate sin, that sin is always punished with death.

On that day, God unleashed His wrath against the sins that He had previously "passed over." In Exodus 12, Israel was set free from bondage in Egypt when an angel of death *passed over* them and struck dead the first-born males of the Egyptians. The death penalty came, in part, to Egypt on account of their sins, while at the same time, God showed forbearance toward Israel.

Similarly, God did not bring physical death to Adam and Eve on the day they sinned in the garden. They did die spiritually, but he showed forbearance toward their physical lives. Not only so, He demonstrates great patience with humanity from generation to generation. How could it be that God so often "passed over" sinners upon whom the death penalty was owed? If He is so righteous, then why didn't He always execute swift judgment when a person sins? After all, "the soul who sins will die" (Ezekiel 18:4). The answer is that God stored up His wrath for the final "pass over" day.

It was no coincidence that Jesus died on the day of the Jewish Passover. Ever since the event described in Exodus 12, Israelites had celebrated the Passover every year on the prescribed day. It had been about fifteen hundred years since the original Passover. But on the chosen day, as the Passover Lamb—Jesus Christ—was killed, God demonstrated His justice. The sins that the children of Adam committed up until that point, and even those that would be committed from that point forward, were punished in the body and blood of the second Adam. One representative Man laid down upon the altar and took all God's stored-up wrath against sin. God's just intolerance for sin was unleashed on that day.

Because His own demands for justice were satisfied on that Passover Day, "at the present time" God freely imputes righteousness to children of Adam without violating His own demands for justice. Justice is satisfied. Wrath is quenched. God demonstrates His righteousness, not by overlooking sin and requiring no punishment, but by punishing sin once and for all in Jesus Christ and then uniting sinners to Him. He is "*just*" because He gave the required death penalty for sin. He is "the justifier of the one who has faith in Jesus" because His love compelled Him to do all this, to demonstrate forbearance toward us who believe, to pass over our sins.

3:27-31   Where then is the boasting? It is excluded. By what kind of law? Of works? No, but by a law of faith. For we maintain that a man is justified by faith apart from works of the Law. Or is God the God of Jews only? Is He not the God of Gentiles also? Yes, of Gentiles also, since indeed God who will justify the circumcised by faith and the uncircumcised through faith is one. Do we then nullify the Law through faith? May it never be! On the contrary, we establish the Law.

Recall that when Paul introduced himself in Romans 1:1-6, he did not want the spotlight. He identified himself as a lowly slave (*doulos*). This, we said, is the great and wonderful destination that each of us should desire for ourselves, to delight in being a slave belonging to God. Even when acknowledging the authority of his role as an apostle who writes the very words of God, Paul wants no glory ascribed to himself, but instead describes his service as being "for [Jesus] name's sake" (1:5). This is because the endgame of the gospel is not just to call forth a people to enjoy heaven forever, but rather, to call forth a people who will *glorify God* in the joy of abiding with Him forever. Christians have long said it well that "the chief end of man is to glorify God, and to enjoy Him forever[3]." The

---

[3] Westminster Shorter Catechism

"law of faith" is consistent with the purpose of God's creation. All things were created *by God* for the purpose of bringing glory *to God*.

God created the nation of Israel in order to have a people that are called by His name, that bring Him glory by living in obedience to His covenants. Israel consistently broke their end of the covenant. But God still gets the glory. That is because God's purpose for Israel was always greater than the people of Israel themselves. They were (and are) a vessel through which God is intent upon glorifying Himself.

God gave the Law to Israel, and although He genuinely desired for them to keep the Law, He always knew that they would not. Nothing in His plan was thwarted by Israel's disobedience, because the Law had a double function. In the first place, it governed morality. But in the second, it exposed every point in which people fell short of God's standards, thus revealing to people that we need God, that we need Him to save us from ourselves. And the Law promised this salvation. Through the graphic image of animal sacrifice and thinly veiled prophecies about the glory to be revealed when Messiah comes, the Law was a tutor that brings people to Christ. By saving disobedient Israel, even everyone who believes in Him, God, not Israel, gets the glory.

The "law of faith" (3:27) is exceedingly better than the Law of works, because it spotlights God. If people could work to earn God's acceptance, they would delight in their own righteous behavior. Is there anything more ugly than a self-righteous person? It offends us to the core to see self-righteousness in others because the deepest part of us (that which is made in the image of God) knows to whom all glory is really due. The prideful man steals glory from God. This is the end result of any religion based on works. The more someone practices it, the more the person gets puffed up. It is a trap.

The Law of works is like a giant hamster wheel for humanity. It keeps people running, straining to obey every moral law. The better a man runs, he grows increasingly impressed by his own effort, especially the harder he sees others fall. In the end, he has gone no farther than anyone else, but he has boasted and offended God's glory all along the way. The delight of a rescued man is not like the one who runs. The one whom God saves from the hamster wheel by the law of faith will forever appreciate God.

The greatest thing about the Law of works is that it established our need for a Savior and promised that He would come. After however long it takes to taste defeat up against that stone cold wall of God's Law, "we establish the Law" (3:31) by agreeing with it that we are lawbreakers. Then when we find rescue from that dead end, we are set forever praising the God who saved us on the basis of the law of faith. There will be no boasting in heaven, except in God and in the cross of our Lord Jesus Christ (Galatians 6:14).

14

Abraham

"But to the one who does not work, but believes in Him who justifies the ungodly, his faith is credited as righteousness"

—*Romans 4:5*

When people seek to glorify themselves, it is an ugly thing, because all glory belongs to God, not to men. But when God seeks to glorify Himself, it is a beautiful thing, because all glory does, in fact, belong to Him. The principle of *justification by faith* is perfectly consistent with the order of the Universe, because when God justifies the ungodly, He receives glory for His saving work. The people God saves did not work for salvation, so we do not receive the glory. Desiring to glorify Himself, God has determined to judge the world on the basis of faith rather than according to our works. To prove that this is indeed the case, it would help if Paul provided an example. It helps that the example he provides is none other than Abraham—the father of the nation of Israel, the father of faith.

4:1-3   What then shall we say that Abraham, our forefather according to the flesh, has found? For if Abraham was justified by works, he has something to boast about, but not before God. For what does the Scripture say?

"Abraham believed God, and it was credited to Him as righteousness."

Did you think that the law of faith was something new? Did you think that the Old Testament revealed a different way of salvation than what we find in New Testament books like the one to the Romans? This is not the case at all! That God gave a Law through Moses does not mean that He saved people on the basis of the record of their obedience to it.

The Old Testament did not advocate a law of works righteousness. It is only *old* in the sense that the fullness of time had not yet come, even the time for Christ to be revealed. Some of the primary promises of the Old Testament were fulfilled in Christ or given a new trajectory when He emerged from the tomb. For example, all the moral laws of Leviticus, even those found in chapter 18, should still direct Christian morality. But just like the Jews when the Law first appeared, our righteousness will not depend on how well we do, but on whether or not God draws from the merits of Christ to credit righteousness to our account. It was the same for the Jews to whom the Law was given, although they didn't understand as much as we do about Christ's righteousness imputed to believers.

But the commands to make sacrifices, observe the dietary code and keep the Sabbath (Exodus 20:8-11) follow a different trajectory under the New Covenant. Jesus accomplished the great and final once-for-all sacrifice when He died on the cross, so we must *not* offer any more blood. Dietary restrictions were lifted as well, in order to demonstrate the lifting of the divide between Jew and Gentile. Peter required a vision to understand that this change had taken place (Acts 10:9-16). With regard to the Sabbath, it is no longer about how much we work on Saturdays, but rather about how we need to stop trying to earn salvation by doing work (Hebrews 4:9-10). Certain aspects of the Law are therefore *old* in the sense of having been fulfilled or having been given a new trajectory.

The Old Testament included the law of faith, but the New Testament revolves around it. The Old Testament visualized the law of faith in things like the Sabbath, even though many Jews never understood the principle. The law of faith is not in opposition to the Old Testament. It is expressed more fully in the New Testament, but it is itself congruent with how God always dealt with His people. Nowhere is it more clearly expressed than in the story of Abraham.

Abraham was called to become a child of God long before God had even given his moral law. That would come later through Moses. But righteousness was imputed to Abraham. On what basis was righteousness credited to Abraham? "Abraham believed God, and it was credited to him as righteousness." This quote from Genesis 15:6 proves that the law of faith was in operation from the beginning. God would later give the Law of Moses to govern morality, to set apart Israel as a distinct nation belonging to God, to make people aware of their sin, and to promise Messiah, among other things. But the law of faith was already operating at the time of Abraham.

Even before this account of Abraham in Genesis 15:6, Adam and Eve accepted God's covering for sin in Genesis 3:21, thus establishing the law of faith. Their trust in the Deliverer promised in Genesis 3:15 (a "seed of the woman" would crush Satan's head) was the key to Adam and Eve being counted as righteous. They certainly didn't attain righteousness by obeying God's command, because they violated the only one they had (Genesis 2:17). They were the first ones to have to wait on that "Seed of a woman" (Genesis 3:15), that descendant of theirs who would make things right for them.

Like all who descend from them, for Adam and Eve, it was their waiting and their *looking*, not their work to make up for what they had done, that ultimately restored righteousness to them. The righteousness of Jesus was accounted to them based on what Jesus would do. The God who exists outside of time is able to apply the benefits of the atonement to people who believe His revelation, regardless of whether they lived in generations preceding or following the once-and-for-all sacrifice of the Messiah.

4:4-8   Now to the one who works, his wage is not credited as a favor, but as what is due. But to the one who does not work, but believes in Him who justifies the ungodly, his faith is credited as righteousness, just as David also speaks of the blessing on the man to whom God credits righteousness apart from works: "Blessed are those whose lawless deeds have been forgiven, and whose sins have been covered. Blessed is the man whose sin the Lord will not take into account."

King David, like Abraham, was a man of faith. Read the Book of Psalms. It is amazing how David pours out his heart to God. His prayers range from the jubilant to the heart wrenching. They are raw and beautiful, at the same time. Even now three thousand years later, the reader will be impressed by how *real* they are. David was a man whose most noteworthy characteristic was his faith.

David was not so good at obeying the Law of Moses. He had a number of moral failures. He had an affair with the wife of one of his best men. Then as part of an effort to cover it up, he had that friend murdered. Uriah, the victim, was an exceedingly righteous man. David had terrible moral failures. He paid dearly in the havoc that it wreaked in his family. But nothing he suffered or did could ever make up for the sins he committed. Uriah was still dead, and David was still guilty of having broken the Law of Moses.

Had David been judged by his works, he would be in hell as we speak. But God dealt with David by the same law of faith that He uses to judge us. David "[believed] in Him who justifies the ungodly" (Romans 4:5). The righteousness of God was imputed to David because David had repentant faith. Notice that David did not do anything to deserve forgiveness. He received it by faith and by faith *alone*.

The gospel is good news that blesses undeserving people. "Blessed are those whose lawless deeds have been forgiven, and whose sins have been covered. Blessed is the man whose sin the Lord will not take into account."

The moralist just cannot accept the law of faith. He is determined to contribute something to the equation. "Surely," he reasons, "I must contribute something to my salvation." The false prophet Joseph Smith, founder of the Mormon religion, even went so far as to rewrite Romans 4:5, literally negating what it says by adding the word "not." Writing exactly the opposite of what Paul wrote, Smith "translated" (without any manuscript evidence) Paul to say, "believeth on him who justifieth **not** the ungodly" (Joseph Smith Translation of Romans 4:5). Smith simply couldn't believe that God "justifies the ungodly."

David was a jubilant worshipper precisely because he believed the law of faith. "Deliver me from blood-guiltiness, O God, the God of my salvation; then my tongue will joyfully sing of your righteousness" (Psalm 51:14). He looked to God. He looked for deliverance, for salvation. He trusted that only the imputation of God's righteousness could make him righteous. So he did not tout his own greatness as a prophet. David was a prophet because God communicated His word to us through David. But David's joyful songs were written to the God who saves and imputes righteousness to "the ungodly" (Romans 4:5). We, like David, are among those who don't deserve to be blessed, whose work has earned us nothing but wrath, but whose faith is credited as righteousness if only we believe in Jesus.

4:9-12   Is this blessing then on the circumcised, or on the uncircumcised also? For we say, "Faith was credited to Abraham as righteousness." How then was it credited? While he was circumcised, or uncircumcised? Not while circumcised, but while uncircumcised; and he received the sign of circumcision, a seal of the righteousness of the faith which he had while uncircumcised, so that he may be the father of all who believe without being circumcised, that righteousness might be credited to them, and the father of circumcision to those who not only are of the circumcision, but who also follow in the steps of the faith of our father Abraham which he had while uncircumcised.

The division between Jew and Gentile was a big deal at the time the book of Romans was written. It is still a fairly big deal today, when you consider how the world continues to be shaped by that tiny sliver of land along the Mediterranean that is Israel. But another amazing thing about the unfolding of God's plan is that Abraham, the father of the nation, lived part of his life as an uncircumcised Gentile and the other as a circumcised Jew. By looking back to him, Jew and Gentile are brought together. All of us stand in need of the same salvation. The righteousness that comes by faith is given, not only to the circumcised Jew, but to all who follow in the steps of the faith of our father Abraham.

4:13-15   For the promise to Abraham or to his descendants that he would be heir of the world was not through the Law, but through the righteousness of faith. For if those who are of the Law are heirs, faith is made void and the promise is nullified; for the Law brings about wrath, but where there is no law, there also is no violation.

God made a special promise to Abraham. Sending him to the Promised Land, God said, "I will make you a great nation, and I will bless you, and make your name great; and so you will be a blessing; and I will bless those who bless you, and the one who curses you I will curse. And in you all the families of the earth will be blessed" (Genesis 12:2-3). The world was indeed blessed in Abraham, because Jesus the Messiah came through Abraham's seed.

So great a promise was not conditioned upon the Law. The birth of Moses and the giving of the Law were still about five hundred years away. So the Law was not an instrument of the promise. The promise was given before the Law and was sure to be fulfilled regardless of who did or did not keep the Law. The faith of Abraham is a different thing altogether from the observance of Torah. Anyone who thinks that he will be justified by keeping the Law is under wrath, because the Law was given to make people aware of places where they fall short of God's glory in order that they would look to God for salvation. We, like Abraham, are not under Law, so there is nothing for us to violate. We are judged according to our faith, just like Abraham was.

4:16-25   For this reason it is by faith, in order that it may be in accordance with grace, so that the promise will be guaranteed to all the descendants, not only to those who are of the Law, but also to those who are of the faith of Abraham, who is the father of us all, (as it is written, "A father of many nations have I made you") in the presence of Him whom he believed, even God, who gives life to the dead and calls into being that which does not exist. In hope against hope he believed, so that he might become a father of many nations according to that which had been spoken, "So shall your descendants be." Without becoming weak in faith he contemplated his own body, now as good as dead since he was about a hundred years old, and the deadness of Sarah's womb; yet, with respect to the promise of God, he did not waver in unbelief, but grew strong in faith, giving glory to God, and being fully assured that what God had promised, He was able also to perform. Therefore it was also credited to him as righteousness. Now not for his sake only was it written that it was credited to him, but for our sake also, to whom it was credited, as those who believe in Him who raised Jesus our Lord from the dead, He who was delivered over because of our transgressions, and was raised because of our justification.

God took Abraham outside and said, "'Now look toward the heavens, and count the stars, if you are able to count them.' And He said to him, 'So shall your descendants be'" (Genesis 15:5). But as years passed and as Abraham and Sarah aged, approaching a hundred years old, the human odds of the promise coming true had disappeared. Nevertheless, Abraham still believed that God would fulfill His promise. And God did.

In the verse that followed the promise, "so shall your descendants be" (Genesis 15:5), Abraham was counted as a righteous man. Notice that God saw Abraham's faith the minute Abraham believed God's promise. "Then he believed in the Lord, and He reckoned it to him as righteousness" (Genesis 15:6). Abraham would persevere in his faith for many years, but righteousness was a gift that came at the front end. It is the same with us. The verse was written "for our sake also" (Romans 4:24).

We are likewise saved the minute we believe in Jesus. For the rest of our lives, we who have genuinely believed will continue to be "fully assured that what God [has] promised, He [is] able also to perform" (Romans 4:21). We will not waver in unbelief, but it is our great privilege to be like Abraham and increase in faith. He "grew strong in faith" (4:20). As the thesis of the book of Romans declares, in the gospel "the righteousness of God is revealed from faith to faith" (Romans 1:17). The point is that from the minute of our salvation—our Genesis 15:6 "but now" (Romans 3:21) moment—until our dying breath when we pass into the very presence of Jesus Christ, we are justified, we are counted righteous, through faith in Jesus Christ.

Abraham had less light than we do. We "believe in Him who raised Jesus our Lord from the dead, He who was delivered over because of our transgressions, and was raised because of our justification" (Romans 4:24-25). Abraham was justified by the same propitiation in the same blood as we are, but his faith was only placed in the amount of revelation that had been given at the time. Nevertheless, the principle of believing the promises of God is the crucial point for us to understand. We who live on this side of history, after Jesus died for our transgressions and rose from the dead, the resurrection showing that the redeeming payment had been made, are justified when we believe the message. God's promise is now eternal life for everyone who believes in Jesus, those who trust the sufficiency of His work.

The work of Christ Jesus was entirely gracious. It was all His doing. It was entirely motivated by the goodness of God's heart. For this reason, God deserves all the glory. The law of *faith* fits perfectly with the concept of *grace*, because faith affords no glory to the one who believes. He has contributed nothing. He only trusts in the ability of Another. The believer thinks that "God [is] able to perform" (Romans 4:21). This trust spotlights God as the Performer. Since faith is all about "giving glory to

God" (4:20), it is "in accordance with grace" (4:16). As the Protestant Reformers loved to say, "Salvation is by *grace* alone through *faith* alone in *Christ* alone according to *Scripture* alone for the *glory of God* alone."

15

Peace

"Therefore, having been justified by faith, we have
peace with God through our Lord Jesus Christ"

—Romans 5:1

Paul often previews material before formally presenting it in a later section of his book. He previewed the good news of the gospel in the middle of a section about the bad news of God's wrath toward our sin (Romans 2:4). Here in a section that delivers the good news about how sinners can be declared righteous, he previews the next section of Romans, which will deal with the new life that begins when a person is declared righteous. The new life will be fully explained in chapters 6-8, but here Paul found it necessary to mention, because the new life comes as a result of justification by faith.

5:1-5   Therefore, having been justified by faith, we have peace with God through our Lord Jesus Christ, through whom also we obtained our introduction by faith into this grace in which we stand, and we exult in the hope of the glory of God. And not only this, but we also exult in our tribulations, knowing that tribulation brings about perseverance, and perseverance, proven character; and proven character, hope; and hope does not disappoint, because the love of God has been poured out within our hearts through the Holy Spirit who was given to us.

If you arrive at this place of being justified by faith, you have reached the destination! You are safely home! We have employed a traveling analogy to learn the meaning of the book of Romans. If we are travelers on the road of life, the book of Romans is our map. First of all, it provides an overview of where we are going (1:1-17). That road is called "the gospel." Then in the first section of the book, it locates us. Our starting point is somewhere deep in the jungle of sin, where we are helplessly lost and too far from home to ever make it on our own (1:18-3:20). "But now" (3:21), in a drastic turn of events, the righteousness of God manifests upon the lost soul who places faith in Jesus Christ. In that moment (*nuni*), the lost is found.

The sinful man who stands helplessly under the wrath of God is justified forever at the moment he believes in Jesus, right where he stands. When we were lost, we always thought that we needed to find our way out of the jungle of sin, to make it home by our own efforts. But through our Lord Jesus Christ, "we have obtained our introduction by faith into this grace *in which we stand*" (5:2). We don't need to go anywhere. We don't need to prove ourselves worthy or earn back anything we squandered. The great surprise of the journey is that salvation has come to meet us where we are.

Justification by faith means that all God's wrath, which the sinner had stored up for the Day of Judgment, has completely vanished. It just isn't there anymore. On the journey of life, the sinner has yet to go anywhere or do anything of merit. And yet here we stand with the benefits of being declared righteous already described in the present tense. "We have peace with God" (5:1). Our relationship with Him is no longer broken. There is no restitution left to be made. When we pray, He gladly listens. All is well between us and Him.

We can rejoice because we are saved in the present tense. "We exult in hope of the glory of God" (5:2). Even though we look around and see a world cursed by sin, we already have the joy of the Lord. Hope is the future-oriented aspect of our faith, and since we have come to believe in Jesus Christ, we are settled in our hearts, knowing that He will work all things out in the end. Since the "love of God has been poured out within our hearts" (5:5), we know that God will one day complete the process of making us the people He wants us to be. But the point is that we are already truly found. We are made alive, having arrived at "this grace in which we stand" (5:2) simply by trusting in Jesus Christ. Salvation has come to meet us where we are.

Notice that the book of Romans roadmap does not say that we are immediately snatched out of the world in which we live. That is not the kind of rescue we received. We are immediately reconciled with God and given His perspective on life, which enables us to exult in Him. That salvation and joy of salvation is an immediate gift. But it is a gift we are to carry with us as we continue on the journey. Because such a drastic change has come over us, it is right to think of ourselves as having become aliens in this world. We still must pass through the jungle of sin with all of its obstacles, but we do so as travelers passing through and as travelers carrying an all-surpassing power with us as we go (2 Corinthians 4:7).

The roadmap says that we "exult in our tribulations" (5:3). This means that we still face a difficult road ahead. But now we know a few things that we didn't before. We know salvation, which previously we did not have. We used to have a fearful expectation of judgment that would one day consume the enemies of God. Even if we attempted to mollify that sense of dread, it was there because it was real. But now we have a deep-seated peace. We already know with certainty where we are going when we die. We also know that the process of going through tribulations is part of how God is going to make us the people He wants us to be. Whatever He allows to come our way on the journey of life, it will be for our character development and transformation into the image of God. So at the moment of salvation, we are immediately given joy in the face of the road that we must travel.

16

Loved

"But God demonstrates His own love toward us, in that while we were yet sinners, Christ died for us"

—*Romans 5:8*

Paul continues to describe the immediate condition of the person who is justified by faith. Such a person is immediately and entirely released from God's wrath, and such a one exults in God, joyfully giving glory to God because the saved man knows what has happened to him. He knows that he has been saved.

Contemplating so great a salvation, the saved person is overwhelmed by the thought of how much God loves him or her. God's love "has been poured out within our hearts." This is why the saved person exults in God, and the book of Romans now helps us to think about how great this love really is.

5:6-11   For while we were still helpless, at the right time Christ died for the ungodly. For one will hardly die for a righteous man; though perhaps for the good man someone would dare even to die. But God demonstrates His own love toward us, in that while we were yet sinners, Christ died for us. Much more then,

> having now been justified by His blood, we shall be
> saved from the wrath of God through Him. For if
> while we were enemies we were reconciled to God
> through the death of His Son, much more, having been
> reconciled, we shall be saved by His life. And not only
> this, but we also exult in God through our Lord Jesus
> Christ, through whom we have now received the
> reconciliation.

It is not just the love of a father who would die in the place of his son. That is the kind of love that I understand, the kind of love with which every good dad can resonate. We would gladly die to save our sons or daughters. But what is this love of God that would give His Son to die in our place? Who are we that He would love us? Are we not made of dust, just the same elements of this world from which everything else was made? Worse than that, are we not the very enemies of God who have broken His righteous commands and preferred the idols of our making to the worship of the Maker of all things? Are we not the wicked ones upon whom the wrath of God *is revealed* from heaven? We may be able to comprehend the love of someone who dies for a righteous man, but from where did God's love come? While we were yet ungodly, unrighteous sinners who suppress the truth in unrighteousness, Christ died for us! This is a demonstration of love that far surpasses anything of which we could have conceived.

The greatness of God's loving gift is underscored by the timing in which it came. Where at one moment we stood condemned and utterly helpless, in the next moment we stood completely justified. God's gift happened at the moment in time when Jesus died on the cross, and in the same way, the gift of salvation is immediately given to individuals in the moment when they receive the offer. God, who exists outside of time, considers the moment of our redemption to be the moment of Christ's death. His death really accomplished our redemption on that day. On the day that we receive the gift, all the benefits of His work on the cross are immediately applied to us.

The love of God is poured out so profusely "at the right time" that the ungodly has "now been" justified. As a result of this present expression of love, it is a certainty that on the Judgment Day—the Day of God's Wrath—we "*shall be* saved from His wrath." Since it is a settled fact that we are protected by the love of God, "having been reconciled," there is no longer any doubt that "we shall be saved by His life." The love of God has been poured out completely upon the believer in Jesus. His love has completely secured the believer's future. The verdict is in. The sinner is declared righteous. Now righteous, he has peace, joy, hope, and most of all, love in Jesus Christ, "through whom we *have now* received the reconciliation (5:11)."

17

Free

"But the free gift is not like the transgression. For if by the transgression of the one the many died, much more did the grace of God and the gift by the grace of the one Man, Jesus Christ, abound to the many"

—Romans 5:15

Having turned the reader's attention to contemplate the love of God and the completeness of salvation that resulted from so great a love, Paul now directs the minds of the reader to think theologically. To set up what he wants to say about the big-picture significance of Christ's one-time act of love, Paul has to remind the reader of how the world came to its present condition.

5:12-14   Therefore, just as through one man sin entered into the world, and death through sin, and so death spread to all men, because all sinned—for until the Law sin was in the world, but sin is not imputed when there is no law. Nevertheless death reigned from Adam until Moses, even over those who had not sinned in the likeness of the offense of Adam, who is a type of Him who was to come.

Sin and death entered the world through Adam and Eve. When they disobeyed a direct command from God (Genesis 2:17), the prescribed death penalty came over their souls. What's more, everyone who proceeded from them, with the exception of the virgin-born Son of God, inherited their sin nature. It is not simply that we all were held responsible for what they did, but rather "because all sinned," we prove that we are just like our parents. Had we been the ones tested in the garden, we likewise would have fallen.

We are all guilty of breaking commands. But what about those who never had commands, the reader wonders. In principle, it is true that without any commands, it is impossible to disobey God. But the evident fact that death has extended its reach to all is proof that all people are lawbreakers. After Adam and Eve were expelled from the garden, the command not to eat of the Tree of the Knowledge of Good and Evil (Genesis 2:17) became impossible to break. The Law of Moses did not come for several thousand years. So what law did the intermittent generations of people break?

When prosecuting God's case against humanity, Paul already said that "the work of the law written on their hearts, their conscience bearing witness" (Romans 2:15) was a law unto them. So, even without a command like Adam had, it is clear that death reigned from the time of Adam until Moses because sin reigned in all of Adam's descendants.

Adam is therefore a representative man, representative of our sinful state of being and representative of the certain result of death. No one should think of themselves as an exception, because since the time of Moses, the world now has the written Law of God governing our morality and exposing every place where we fall short. Even if a person has no access to that mirror, they are condemned nonetheless by actions that deviate from law of conscience. People harden their hearts against God, their consciences being seared as with a hot iron, but so it is to be *given over* to sin. All the descendants of Adam are like Adam in being given over to sin, managing to stay above the earth for only a short time before joining those who went before them into the dust from which Adam was made.

5:15-17   But the free gift is not like the transgression. For if by the transgression of the one the many died, much more did the grace of God and the gift by the grace of the one Man, Jesus Christ, abound to the many. The gift is not like that which came through the one who sinned; for on the one hand the judgment arose from one transgression resulting in condemnation, but on the other hand the free gift arose from many transgressions resulting in justification. For if by the transgression of the one, death reigned through the one, much more those who receive the abundance of grace and of the gift of righteousness will reign in life through the One, Jesus Christ.

Here again, justification by faith is presented as a stark contrast to what has gone before it. Romans 1:18-3:20 presented the helpless condition of the lost. Romans 3:21 broke in with a "but now" manifestation of God's righteousness. As Paul would have us continue to contemplate this glorious truth, he draws our attention to the reign of death that has persisted from the time of Adam. But breaking in to rescue us from the falling away ("transgression", παράπτωμα, paraptoma, means a lapse, slip, or false step) and from the death that came as a result, a free gift appears.

Two contrasts and one comparison help us to think about how great the gift really is. By way of comparison, we see that even as death entered through one man, so also the gift entered through one Man. The Hebrew name Adam simply means "man", and Jesus is thus the second Adam. There is a one-to-one parallel between how sin entered the world and how it receives its remedy. Both came through only one man.

But, whereas the first Adam failed just one time and that was enough to bring death to all, in contrast, all the failings of all the descendants of Adam could not stop and indeed even called forth the arising of the free gift that results in justification. One little sin brought death to all, but one glorious gift overwhelms even all the sins of all who ever were.

The second contrast, though, discriminates between the universally guilty human race and that particular people "who receive" the gift. This contrast is so important. Dear reader, please understand that even though Jesus Christ died for the sins of the world, offering a free gift that extends to all, it will only be applied to those "who receive the abundance of grace and of the gift." People can remain passive, do nothing, and they will certainly fall under the reign of death. Death reigns. It does so no matter what you do. But to "reign in life," by contrast ("much more" denotes a great overcoming, not a heightening of the same thing), requires that you "receive" (λαμβάνω, lambano, means "I get", "I take", or "I lay hold of") the gift. You must take hold of the gift, not by doing anything for God, but by trusting God, by receiving in faith.

Dear reader, you can do that right now. Simply pray. Tell God that this is what you want. Ask Him to apply His gift of righteousness to you. Confess your sins to Him, acknowledging that the just penalty of sin rightfully hangs over your head. Admit that you deserve death. Then thank Him for the gift of Jesus Christ, the second Adam, whose death at Calvary overwhelmed the reign of death. Ask Him, Jesus Christ, to come into your life. Tell Him that you receive Him by faith and gladly take hold of the gift He offers. Say yes to His offer of grace.

If you have just called on Jesus to save you, asking sincerely from your heart, then what could stop Him from answering your call? The second Adam died for this very thing. "For God so loved the world that He gave His only begotten Son, that whoever believes in Him shall not perish, but have eternal life. For God did not send the Son into the world to judge the world, but that the world might be saved through Him. He who believes in Him is not judged; he who does not believe has been judged already, because he has not believed in the name of the only begotten Son of God" (John 3:16-18).

You needed to do nothing to be a son of Adam, to be under the reign of death. But by receiving the gift of the Second Adam, it is promised that you will reign in life. This receiving is not *work*, but only the trust of a person who knows the unworthiness of his or her own work and therefore depends upon the One who accomplished every necessary work on our behalf.

5:18-21   So then as through one transgression there resulted condemnation to all men, even so through one act of righteousness there resulted justification of life to all men. For as through the one man's disobedience the many were made sinners, even so through the obedience of the One the many will be made righteous. The Law came in so that the transgression would increase; but where sin increased, grace abounded all the more, so that, as sin reigned in death, even so grace would reign through righteousness to eternal life through Jesus Christ our Lord.

"So then" indicates Paul's intention to summarize and draw this glorious section of his epistle to a close. We have seen what every sinner needs to see. We have seen a manifestation of God's righteousness, which is what it takes to be "good enough" in God's eyes. If we have obeyed the text, we recognize that righteousness is imputed to those who place their faith in Jesus Christ. Justification by faith is the doctrine that reveals the way to be saved.

There is one way to be saved offered by one Man who did one thing. The first man's single act of disobedience was the instrument through which each of us became a sinner. But it is our own sin for which we are condemned. The fact is that God has given the Law through Moses, and we break it. Our lawbreaking means, by definition, that we are sinners. Every instance where we break a rule only increases our guilt. So "sin reigns in death." "But now" (3:21) a way of salvation is offered to us. It is the only way.

As Jesus said, "I am the way, and the truth, and the life; no one comes to the Father but through Me" (John 14:6). No "one" will make it on their own because "the many were made sinners" in Adam. But "the One" was obedient, even obedient unto death, even death on a cross. This "one act of righteousness," the Messiah sacrificially giving His innocent lifeblood unto death, opens the way of salvation to all who come "through Jesus Christ our Lord."

It is essential to remember that "through one act of righteousness there resulted justification of life to all men." Since the one-time sacrifice of Jesus provided redemption, it is a flagrant offense to the God of the gospel to say that priests today can offer propitiatory sacrifices on an altar. When a Roman Catholic priest acts as if he is another Christ and claims that his work at the altar renders the body and blood of Jesus really present in the Eucharist, the priest has denied our text (5:18-21). He has devalued the real blood that Jesus poured out to pay for redemption, the blood that served as a propitiation to appease God's wrath. He has essentially told the people that the sacrifice of Jesus on the cross was *not enough*. The priest has inserted himself between the sinner and the God who justifies sinners by faith. This is such a flagrant offense that it is right to characterize Rome's gospel as a false gospel, because it opposes the main idea of the gospel, which is justification through faith.

The third section of the book of Romans (3:21-5:21) brings salvation to us right where we stand. After the Overview (1:1-1:17), the second section (1:18-3:20) located us in the jungle of sin. We were helplessly lost. But the name "Jesus" means "God Saves," and the third section is a manifestation of His righteousness. As it turns out, there was no way for us to make it out of the jungle, so love came down. God gave a gift by His grace, even Jesus Christ publicly sacrificed, spilling His blood in our place. The One Man did this one thing and opened a way for us to be saved.

When a sinner comes to believe in Jesus, the Savior meets the sinner wherever he or she is. No matter how entangled in the vines of sin. No matter how deep in the mud of shame. Jesus appears and unites Himself with the sinner. The righteousness of the One is imputed to the other.

Eternal life is available here and now, right where we are. It includes immediate peace with God. It brings joy, even in the midst of the jungle where saved people must continue to tread until God calls us home. The troubles we face here will be for the refining of our character and will bring glory to God as we endure them. God doesn't snatch us out of the world, but everything changes the moment He meets us. He comes and manifests His righteousness upon us in the very moment we believe in Jesus Christ. Justification comes through faith, and so the journey begins.

SECTION 4

Seeing Ourselves as Good
Romans 6-8

18

Baptisms

"Therefore we have been buried with Him through baptism into death,
so that as Christ was raised from the dead through the glory of the
Father, so we too might walk in newness of life"

—Romans 6:4

The fourth section of the book of Romans begins with a Christian standing still in the jungle of sin. Before he gets moving, he looks around and takes in his surroundings. The world is the same, but it looks totally different. What used to be just a few trees now looks like a million-square-mile jungle of sin. He finally sees it as it is because God did something to show him. God has inserted a mirror before the eyes of the lost man. Romans 1:18-3:20 has dropped into the sinner's view and changed the way the man thinks about sin. He was horrified by what he saw in the mirror of God's law, and he knows the same sad reality describes the plight of everyone else he sees in the jungle. He has a new view of the world.

But at the moment our sinner took an honest look in the mirror, a glorious light burst forth from heaven. It encompassed the man. This light of the gospel (3:21-5:21) enveloped him in an alien righteousness—the righteousness of Christ imputed to the man on account of the man's faith. At once, peace flooded his soul, and he began to exult in God. He still sees the difficulty of the road that lies ahead. But now that he knows he is right with God, he is convinced that everything else will surely be okay. He has seen the glory of Jesus Christ.

As the man on the Romans Road enters the next stage of his journey, described in Romans 6-8, we remember that this is our journey too. So far we have been just standing still. We stood condemned under the wrath of God (1:18-3:20). Then in a glorious moment, we were transformed right where we stood. We were justified by faith in Jesus Christ (5:1) "through whom also we have obtained our introduction by faith into this grace in which we stand" (5:2a).

God's kindness came to us in an expression of love the likes of which the world has never seen. "While we were yet sinners, Christ died for us" (5:8b). Though we had not made so much as a gesture toward God, nor gone anywhere or done anything for God, God met us at our point of need and saved us. That salvation, we will now discover, has changed everything. It is almost time to get moving, but first we must see ourselves anew.

We need to see ourselves differently now that we have been saved. This time the mirror has been set aside. The mirror will remain with us, and we need to return to it from time to time, because nothing in the Old Testament will pass away or cease to serve a function, but the mirror of the Law will no longer define us. From the moment of our salvation, we are no longer to view ourselves as sinners who break the Law. We are no longer under Law. Here now, we have become saints (1:7). We need to look carefully and recognize that in Christ, we are good. We need to see ourselves as good.

There is a pool of water at our feet. Before we disturb its stillness, we need to gather an image of ourselves from the reflection it provides. This is the fourth section of the book of Romans, and it is here to show you a vision of a new you, before you go anywhere or do anything.

6:1-7   What shall we say then? Are we to continue in sin so that grace may increase? May it never be! How shall we who died to sin still live in it? Or do you not know that all of us who have been baptized into Christ Jesus have been baptized into His death? Therefore we have been buried with Him through baptism into death, so that as Christ was raised from the dead through the glory of the Father, so we too might walk in newness of life. For if we have become united with Him in the likeness of His death, certainly we shall also be in the likeness of His resurrection, knowing this, that our old self was crucified with Him, in order that our body of sin might be done away with, so that we would no longer be slaves to sin; for he who has died is freed from sin.

What do we say (and think) about ourselves now that our faith has brought us completely into the grace in which we stand? Since nothing is required of us to earn salvation, should we just go on sinning the way we did before we were saved? What's more, if God's grace results in His receiving glory (Romans 5:2-8), in that His willingness to forgive demonstrates His perfect and most beautiful love, then why don't we just go ahead and sin heartily so that God has a lot to forgive? More sin simply means more glory to God.

"May it never be!" God rejects this view of *the new you* as emphatically as language will allow. The Apostle shouts "no" (μή, mé), the strongest Greek word available to say that the believer must never think of his present and future life in that way. The Greek word *mé* completely rules out all possibilities associated with the thought.

The believer is to envision *the new you* as a resurrected being. The old man is dead and buried. The quality of life of the person to whom the righteousness of God has manifested is now entirely new. The person is truly alive for the first time. The living being, like Adam and Eve before the fall, does not live to eat the forbidden fruit of the Tree of the Knowledge of Good and Evil. He lives to glorify God and enjoy the garden the Lord has provided. There is a kind of innocence to the new creation.

To be sure, the believer still must live in the jungle. God allows the memory of sin to remain in the believer's brain. The trees of temptation are still everywhere to be seen. A deceitful tempter is still lurking and looking for opportunities. But the believer must now develop a keen sense of *not belonging* in the world. He must look intently into the fourth section of Romans and see himself as a righteous pilgrim sojourning in a wicked place. He must think of himself as belonging to the garden, as only being home when in a place where there is no sin. Although he knows himself prone to stumble in a world of sin, he must see himself as already being a citizen of the Kingdom of Light. He must see *a vision of a new you* instead of focusing on his surroundings.

Paul employs a metaphor to drive this vision into the mind of the new Christian. *Baptism* in water is a symbolic act that demonstrates the reality this passage describes. The word "baptism" (βάπτισμα, baptisma) means to immerse, such as in the dipping or submersion of cloth into a dye to infuse the cloth with color. Even as that immersion will come to identify the cloth that emerges from it, so also the *meaning* of baptism is *identification*. The believer has been *placed into* Christ. His whole life is now defined by what Christ has accomplished for him and in him. Baptism is all about *identification*. Something or someone is *identified* as having been *placed into* something or Someone else.

In the New Testament, the word "baptism" is used in association with different objects to which someone needs to *identify*. There are different things that someone may need to be *placed into*. Jesus talks about the baptism of suffering (Matthew 20:22) whereby He would be *placed into* the suffering of crucifixion, even drenched in His own blood, in order to *identify* Himself with sinners and die an atoning death in our stead.

Speaking through John the Baptist, God promises a baptism with the Holy Spirit and fire (Matthew 3:11, Luke 3:16), a better baptism than that of repentance found in the waters of the Jordan under the hands of John. This baptism is not only able to *identify* one's repentance in the eyes of others but to actually *accomplish* it in the heart of the baptized, changing the heart of the baptized into a passionate flame of worship (Matthew 3:11, Luke 3:16). The fire-baptized man is a new creation, the old having been consumed by the Spirit's fire and the new displaying the light and warmth of that holy fire, especially in how he loves.

Fire baptism actually *places a believer into Christ* by immersing the person in the Spirit of Christ. The fire of the Holy Spirit envelops the believer. The Spirit's fire never burns out, even if we sometimes begin to quench it (1 Thessalonians 5:19). Immersing a person in the Holy Spirit means *identifying* the person with Christ forever in the sight of God. It is a real change of *identity* that only happens when a person is actually being *placed into* Christ, a change that takes place at the moment of salvation, the moment that a person is justified through faith. Fire baptism accomplishes a real work on the human heart and is therefore what we need to be saved. Jesus administers it (Luke 3:16) when we submit to Him in the obedience of faith (Romans 1:5, 3:21-5:21).

In addition to baptisms of suffering (Matthew 20:22), John's baptism of repentance (Luke 3:16, Acts 19:3) and the baptism of the Holy Spirit and fire (Luke 3:16), there are still other baptisms in the New Testament, all of which serve the purpose of *identification*. When Jesus was baptized—i.e., *placed into* water only to emerge—two unique things happened. The Father *identified* His Son with His voice from heaven, "this is My beloved Son, in whom I am well pleased" (Matthew 3:17), and the Holy Spirit "descended upon Him in bodily form like a dove" (Luke 3:22).

Baptism was clearly to *identify* Jesus as God, thus revealing the Trinity more clearly than had ever been seen before. The baptismal formula given in Matthew 28:19 likewise *identifies* us with the God who is Triune.

Furthermore, the New Testament tells us about a baptism into Moses. When Israel moved under the cloud and crossed under the Red Sea, they were released from bondage in Egypt. The old was gone, and they were *placed into* Moses' care. From that moment on, the nation was *identified* with Moses. In that sense, they were "baptized into Moses" (1 Corinthians 10:2). Israel was *identified* with Moses, who served as a type of our Savior. We are identified with Christ in the same way that Israel was identified with Moses, "so that we would no longer be slaves to sin" (Romans 6:7).

Baptism is also used in other texts to *identify* Christians with other aspects of the Christian life. All genuine Christians have the baptism of the Spirit in the sense of having been born of the Spirit (John 3:3), but the terms of Spirit baptism are also used to *identify* believers with the *power* of the Spirit, to denote when a Christian is *placed into* the operation of some of the Spirit's gifts to the church (Acts 8:17). Similarly, Spirit baptism is spoken of in terms of *identifying* someone with the church as someone who has been *placed into* the community of the Spirit (1 Corinthians 12:13). Baptism always identifies.

The baptism of the Spirit and fire is the most profound baptism that Christians undergo. That is clear from how John juxtaposes his own water baptism in a way that diminishes the significance of water and elevates the importance of fire (Luke 3:16). The point is that man can wash the outside of the body with water, but only God can truly clean and even transform the heart. Spirit baptism is also clearly our most important baptism because being given the one Spirit to drink makes us one body (1 Co. 12:13) and empowers us to do God's work in the world (1 Co. 12:27-31). What could be more important than inclusion in the family of God and empowerment to accomplish His mission?

The other baptism that all Christians need to undergo is water baptism. Fire baptism actually saves, but if the heart of a person has truly been changed into that of a believer (Acts 8:37), then he or she will be willing to go under the water (Acts 8:36). Any pool of water will do. Mature believers will want to make sure a person has genuinely become a believer before baptizing them. In the case of children, the baptizer will want to wait until the child is old enough to really understand. Regardless of age, the baptizer should look for a believable confession, one in which the baptizer has no reason to doubt that the person really believes. That doesn't mean that the believer has to prove his merits by performing good works. It requires wisdom in the baptizer, but the new believer's confession of Christ must not appear forced or fake.

Since there is a human element involved in water baptism, since it requires a human baptizer, since disabilities or a lack of a pool of water or extreme cold or other circumstances could prevent water baptism from taking place for a time, even an extended time, and since salvation is a free gift offered solely on the basis of believing the gospel (3:21-5:21), it should never be said that *water* baptism is an instrument through which God actually saves. God saves by Spirit baptism, an activity of the Spirit, not by an activity of man, prescribed for us though it is.

Water baptism cannot save. This point is conclusively established by the fact that Paul subordinates the importance of water baptism to the preaching of the gospel (1 Corinthians 1:17). If water baptism were part of the gospel, in the sense of being an aspect of saving faith (the gospel does include justification by faith), then Paul could not contrast his preaching of the gospel with baptizing people. But that is what Paul does in 1 Corinthians 1:17.

What's more, the Holy Spirit fire baptized people as they heard and believed the gospel (Acts 10:44), and this event was both temporally and logically *prior to* the water baptism that would follow (10:47-48). Fire-baptized people no longer need saving. So believers are saved before they go into the water.

Paul labored to show that justification is *only* by faith (Romans 3:21-5:21). Baptism is a work. Something is a "work" if it is a religious ritual or any kind of effort that one must contribute in order to be justified. Something does not necessarily require much physical exertion in order to be a "work." In the case of circumcision, the recipient is passive. Nevertheless, the Bible warns, "that if you receive circumcision, Christ will be of no benefit to you" (Galatians 5:2). In the context of the book of Galatians, certain troublemakers had lost the doctrine of "justification by faith" when they added the work of circumcision to their plan of salvation. Likewise, to make water baptism part and parcel of justification by faith is to reintroduce a work that does not belong there.

When in a different context, Peter says "baptism now saves you" (1 Peter 3:21), he immediately distinguishes between the physical water that washes away dirt and the heart of faith that calls for cleansing. Peter says, "not the removal of dirt from the flesh, but an appeal to God for a good conscience" (1 Peter 3:21). Peter distinguishes between outward symbol and inward reality. The counterpart that represents salvation (baptism) must not be confused for the thing itself.

Just as Old Testament sacrifices only saved Israelites in so far as they symbolized the one-time sacrifice of Jesus, so also baptism only saves us in so far as it represents a true believer's faith. A true believer already has a heart of faith before going into the water. That faith already brought justification (Romans 3:21-26). But we who believe must learn to see ourselves as being good in Christ (Romans 6-8). Water baptism is an important step toward that "good conscience" (1 Peter 3:21). The memory of our own baptism (Romans 6:3) will provide us with a symbol for the rest of our lives that will continue to help us reckon ourselves as dead to sin and alive in Christ (Romans 6:11).

Spirit baptism actually saves believers because "God saves" (Yahweh is salvation), and the Spirit is God. Water baptism *identifies* the Christian by an outward *symbolism* that testifies that the inward baptism of the Spirit *has placed* a man in Christ. "If you believe with all your heart" (Acts 8:37), meaning that a genuine inward change of heart has taken place, then it is time to symbolize that internal fire baptism with an external proclamation of it, by simply being *placed into* water. Once someone makes such a visible public declaration as water baptism, the world will begin to take note of the difference that Christ makes in him. Baptism identified the believer, so let him be careful to be known for his love.

Paul's major point in Romans 6:1-7 is that believers have been *placed into* Christ, so we must *identify* ourselves correctly as people who have newness of life. Christ is in us. We must not think of ourselves as people who just go on sinning. Whether Paul had in mind the baptism of fire that actually changes a heart or the baptism in water that symbolizes a change in heart is not knowable. Since the latter is the symbol of the former, in both cases, the point remains. If the believer is *placed into* Christ and *identified* with Christ, then the old man who sins heartily is dead and the new man has a totally new quality of life. We walk in newness of life because we are really *in* Christ and forever *identified* with Him.

Paul assumes all the Roman Christians to whom he writes have been water baptized, so he illustrates his larger point on that basis. But his words also bear witness to believers today that each of us needs to take that first step of obedience. How can we count ourselves dead to sin and alive to God if we are unwilling to submit to the very symbol of our death and resurrection with Christ that He gave us? Every genuine believer should be baptized in water and learn to consider himself dead to sin.

The believer's first step in the jungle of this world is not *out* but *down*, down into the water of baptism. The pool of water (Romans 6-8) will reflect a different identity than the one reflected in the mirror of God's Law (1:18-3:20). Water baptism is the perfect symbolism. Wherever the believer goes from that day on, he will remember who he is. He is a resurrected man, alive with the very life of Christ. The old man is dead and buried. He has emerged from water to walk in newness of life. He is truly alive because the Spirit burns in his heart.

19

Commands

*"Even so consider yourselves to be dead to
sin, but alive to God in Christ Jesus"*

—Romans 6:11

The first commands in the book of Romans appear at this point in the
text. Until now, there were only things that we needed to see and
believe. To believe is a form of obedience, but it is not an activity. It is not
something for us to go forth and do. "The obedience of faith" (Romans
1:5) is simply to accept what is true. The gospel is sort of an implied
command. But it is not presented as a command, lest we think that by our
obedience we contributed something to our salvation. Instead it is
presented as good news that ought to be gladly received. If we thought we
accomplished any good work that brought any merit to the table, then the
gospel would not be a gift of God's grace. We would steal from God's
glory, which glory the gospel jealously reserves for God. But once saved,
we become God's children, and begin to receive commands from our
Father.

6:8-11   Now if we have died with Christ, we believe that we
            shall also live with Him, knowing that Christ, having
            been raised from the dead, is never to die again; death

> no longer is master over Him. For the death that He
> died, He died to sin once for all; but the life that He
> lives, He lives to God. Even so consider yourselves to
> be dead to sin, but alive to God in Christ Jesus.

There are no commands in the book of Romans until chapter 6 because we don't have to do anything to be justified through faith. To receive good news isn't work. It only takes work to reject something that is true. That would be like holding a beach ball under water. The idolater must exert great mental energy to concoct self-deceiving images of reality to justify the false claims that he or she so desperately wants to be true. It is disobedient to the Truth of Jesus Christ to suppress the knowledge of Him when someone preaches the gospel. All unbelievers are already guilty of suppressing knowledge of God's divine nature and eternal power (Romans 1:20-21) and are thus disobedient to the truth. But to reject gospel preaching is doubly disobedient.

This is why Paul can say that God is now "declaring" (ἀπαγγέλλω, apaggelló), or announcing, that everyone should repent of truth suppression (Acts 17:30). It is actually good news to hear that one no longer needs to work so hard suppressing the truth about oneself and God. So repentance and faith are implied commands of the gospel, but they take no work to obey.

Because of the cross, where the price of redemption was paid for in blood, the commands of God are for the growth of believers. They are not addressed to unbelievers as a way of salvation. For example, Jesus' command to "love your neighbor as yourself" (Matthew 22:39) will not benefit the unbeliever who strives to keep it. This command is also part of the Law (Leviticus 19:18). Unbelievers cannot keep it, let alone bear up under all the weight of all the commands of the Law. So, they do not need more commands, but only *good news*.

New Testament commands are for believers. Even the Apostle Peter's command to his Jewish audience to "repent and be baptized" in his first public sermon following the outpouring of the Holy Spirit on the Day of Pentecost (Acts 2:38) was given to believers. God wanted the believing ones among those hearers of the gospel in that unique situation to obey. It appears that the immediate *identification* of the first three thousand churchmen who accepted the gospel that day was the party God planned for the church's birthday. They were baptized "because of" (εἰς, eis) the forgiveness of sin.

They obeyed the command to "listen to these words" (Acts 2:22). But that's not what saved them. They heard the gospel of Jesus, the Lord and Christ, crucified and risen (Acts 2:36), and since the Spirit pierced them to the heart (2:37), they *believed* and were immediately justified by faith. This was the invisible saving work of the Spirit. When Peter then commanded, "repent and be baptized" (2:38), these believing ones gladly and obediently got in line to be baptized. Peter did not command unbelievers to come get saved in water. He commanded believers, who had only been saved for a few moments, to come introduce the church to the world. For the sake of the believer's growth, he commanded them to come and publicly identify with Christ.

It was also for the sake of the world, because in that immediate public display the world got to see 3,000 symbols of the death, burial, and resurrection of Jesus. That explains why Peter and the Apostles didn't take weeks to interview all the potential converts before offering them the waters of baptism. Israel was gathered to Jerusalem for the Feast of Pentecost, so the time was right to allow baptism to serve its intended purpose. Water baptism is a symbol that testifies of the resurrection of Jesus Christ, so allow the symbol to give its representation.

But Paul's first command in the book of Romans is not to go get into the water. In fact, there is no command to baptize given in Romans, even though Romans is God's great treatise on the gospel. The doctrine of salvation hangs upon the structure of this book, so it is safe to say that water baptism is not essential to salvation. Rather, Paul assumes that water baptism has already happened to the believing ones in Rome, and if it had not for some of the newer believers, this is not Paul's pressing concern. Rather it is the *meaning* of baptism that concerns Paul. What then are the earliest commands in the book of Romans?

Paul's **first** command is to identify with the once-crucified forever-risen Jesus and "consider yourselves to be dead to sin, but alive to God in Christ Jesus" (Romans 6:11). Jesus died once and now lives forever. To the believer Paul now commands the same: think of yourself as having once died to a life of sin and as being now forever alive to God. The command is "to consider," which means that as Christians we must actively control our thoughts. We are not yet commanded to go out and do anything. Instead we are commanded to think a certain way. If the thought seems unnatural, then it must be inserted as a kind of self-talk. We must intentionally contemplate this truth as God has given it. Write it on your hand, memorize it, set a reminder on your phone, or do whatever is necessary to think this thought. Continually return to these verses to let them wash you, to clean away false thinking. Obedience to Romans 6:11 requires not just a one-time act of baptism, but a new way of thinking for the rest of life.

Think the thought that is commanded of us. I am dead to sin, and I live for Jesus Christ. Christ will never again die, so sin and death must stay dead in me. Christ is alive forever, so my spirit is alive forever with Him.

6:12-14   Therefore do not let sin reign in your mortal body so that you obey its lusts, and do not go on presenting the members of your body to sin as instruments of unrighteousness; but present yourselves to God as those alive from the dead, and your members as instruments of righteousness to God. For sin shall not be master of you, for you are not under law but under grace.

The **second** command in Romans is a derivative of the first. As a man thinks, so he will do. If we think that we are dead to sin, then we will not grant allowances to our flesh to go ahead and commit a sin. The word "therefore" ties the following command to what preceded it. Since you think of yourself as having been buried with Christ in baptism, obedience to the command follows. "Do not let sin reign." How could we allow ourselves to be mastered by sins of our flesh? The old man, who naturally lived according to the flesh, is dead!

The **third** command reveals that to do so, to go on living under the reign of sin, would be like going to the altar of a false god and presenting your body parts. It would be a deliberate act and a horrific betrayal. We are commanded not to "go on presenting" our bodies to another god. The true God has redeemed us at the price of the blood of His Son and delivered us into the freedom of being a *doulos* to Him. So, our Lord gives us a direct command. "Do not" return to your old cruel taskmaster. "Sin" may entice you with attractive appeals. But you are commanded not to use your mortal bodies as instruments of unrighteousness in service to her. God says that we belong to Him, and we must therefore check into work each day at His feet, presenting ourselves only to Him.

The **fourth** command, therefore, is to "present yourselves to God as those alive from the dead." The activity to which we are commanded is the act of reporting for duty. The attitude of the heart of the one reporting is "as those alive from the dead." We kneel at God's throne with enormous thankfulness and are eager to do His bidding. Our Lord (Master) is the very One who saved us from the wrath that was rightfully stored up against us. He rescued us from the wage of sin, which is death, even from an eternal separation from God in a place of conscious suffering. How gladly ought we to do everything that our Lord asks of us! We present ourselves for service to the very One who saved us.

We gladly give the members of our bodies as instruments to serve Him. We would even die physically in service to Him because being "alive from the dead" includes resurrection after physical death. And we delight to hear God's victorious decree spoken over us. It is humbling to see that He is jealous for our devotion, and it is inspiring to hear His confidence in our whole-hearted obedience. He says, "Sin shall not be master of you."

We are emboldened by His proclamation of the way things are to be going forward. But we are at the same time terrified, knowing that in our foolishness we may inexplicably return to sin from time to time and that such a thing would violate the very order of the universe. Revealing just what kind of Lord He really is to us, God winds up this series of commands with a reminder that reassures us—stumble though we may— the transaction whereby the price of our redemption was paid and we came to belong to Him has been fully completed. There is no way that a genuine servant of God could ever fall from grace and ultimately wind up back under the reign of sin and the wrath of God, because "you are not under Law but under grace."

20

Slaves

"Do you not know that when you present yourselves to someone as slaves for obedience, you are slaves of the one whom you obey, either of sin resulting in death, or of obedience resulting in righteousness?"

—*Romans 6:16*

There are two different paths in the jungle of sin. One is called law. The other is called grace. Law leads a person deeper and deeper into the jungle of sin. The harder a person works to keep the law, the more the law reveals that he is a slave to sin. The end of this road is death. Grace rescues a person from the jungle. It imputes righteousness to a person right where he stands. Life begins before the person goes anywhere in the jungle and is guaranteed to continue even when the person physically dies. Death has no sting, since it is only the moment of eternal rescue from the temporary sojourn that the pilgrim was making through the jungle.

The Grace-Righteousness-Life road ultimately turns upward into heaven. But the Law-Sin-Death road never escapes the jungle (Romans 5:20-21). Since the distinction between law and grace is at the heart of the gospel, the gospel has an answer for those who are on the wrong road. Let's call the ones who are trying hard to get somewhere on the road called law "moralists." Moralists constantly have a finger to point at those of us who travel on the road called grace. When they see sin in our lives, they are offended to the core at our gospel, which proclaims that we are forgiven even when they are not. They think that our road (the gospel) is a dead end. They think that without being under law, there is no restraint to keep us from sinning. What they don't understand is that the road called grace is an "[obedience] from the heart to that form of teaching" that is powerful enough to transform the heart of the one who obeys it.

The *obedience of faith* (Romans 1:5) is only a glad reception of good news. But paradoxically, it produces in the heart of the receiver a willing submission to the will of the Master that far surpasses all the moral striving of the man who thinks that his obedience to God's commands is his hope of salvation. With one's own eternal soul at stake, wouldn't one think that the moralist would behave better than someone who receives eternal life up front as a gift? But grace actually produces higher morality than law does.

When it comes to worldly wealth, we certainly admire the self-made millionaire more than a man who inherited that much wealth. Surely the good works of the moralist esteem him in the eyes of God! On the contrary, the gospel says that God considers those goods works as valuable as filthy rags. "For all of us have become like one who is unclean, and all our righteous deeds are like a filthy garment" (Isaiah 64:6). So, the good behavior of the moralist doesn't impress God at all, but God receives the righteous actions of someone who has faith in Jesus Christ the Lord as being good service. He is pleased with His servant.

Justification by faith means that people are saved by believing in Jesus rather than by being good people who do good works and not too many bad works. The world may think this is the Christian's own man-made excuse for our sins, our own imagined license to sin. But brothers and sisters in Christ, we must not think this way too! We must willingly submit ourselves to God as slaves who joyfully obey God.

6:15-19   What then? Shall we sin because we are not under law but under grace? May it never be! Do you not know that when you present yourselves to someone as slaves for obedience, you are slaves of the one whom you obey, either of sin resulting in death, or of obedience resulting in righteousness? But thanks be to God that though you were slaves to sin, you became obedient from the heart to that form of teaching to which you were committed, and having been freed from sin, you became slaves of righteousness. I am speaking in human terms because of the weakness of your flesh. For just as you presented your members as slaves to impurity and to lawlessness, resulting in further lawlessness, so now present your members as slaves to righteousness, resulting in sanctification.

"Shall we sin because we are not under Law but under grace?" The Apostle Paul reasons with our minds, and he appeals to our hearts. He reminds us that we received a gift from the Lord, and since the Lord is our Master, it follows that we ought to obey Him. Paul pokes at our hearts, reminding us of the peace that Jesus gave and the joy we experienced when we exulted in the God of our salvation (Romans 5:1-5). On the basis of how obedience to the gospel affected our hearts, and because of what our minds tell us about the natural submission that should characterize a servant's approach to his master, the apostle now issues the earlier command (Romans 6:12) once again. You are now on Grace Road, so "present your members as slaves to righteousness." We are not commanded this way in order to give us a road of obedience that would bring us to a place of belonging to God. Rather, we obey God because in the gospel He has already said that we do belong to Him.

We have been set apart for lifelong service to the Lord Jesus. As we obey the repeated command to *present ourselves* for service, this reality is driven home to us and becomes more and more true of how we actually live our lives. Presenting ourselves for service has the benefit of *"resulting in sanctification"* (6:19). This *sanctification* (ἁγιασμός, hagiasmos) refers to being set apart to God and to undergoing the process of becoming holy. This is why God calls us "saints" (Romans 1:7). He has claimed us as His own and made us His holy ones. So now as we think of ourselves the right way, as His holy slaves, we present ourselves time and again to God. Our words, thoughts, and deeds in our daily lives increasingly match the reality of who we really are.

6:20-23   For when you were slaves of sin, you were free in regard to righteousness. Therefore what benefit were you then deriving from the things of which you are now ashamed? For the outcome of those things is death. But now having been freed from sin and enslaved to God, you derive your benefit, resulting in sanctification, and the outcome, eternal life. For the wages of sin is death, but the free gift of God is eternal life in Christ Jesus our Lord.

Even the moralist who thinks he is storing up good things in heaven is actually nothing but a slave to sin. He is in that sense "free in regard to righteousness." He has none of it, even if he thinks he does. He might as well say, "Let us eat and drink, for tomorrow we die" (1 Corinthians 15:32). In that sense, anyone who has not been justified by faith in Christ is actually the one with a "license to sin!"

It could be that more sin will result in a worse condition in hell (if like in Dante's Inferno, sin yields different degrees of punishment), but it is certain that apart from the saving grace of the Second Adam, every person is going to hell anyway. On their way to hell, people are "free in regard to righteousness." Righteous deeds impute no benefit to the one who is already guilty and condemned under the penalty of death.

In this passage Paul asks the Christian what was so great about life in slavery to sin. It was leading straight to hell! Then he shows the alternative to be so much better. Slavery to sin had no benefit, but if someone switches masters and becomes enslaved to God instead, there is great benefit. That benefit is two-fold. First, *sanctification* begins to take place immediately. As the believer "presents his members as slaves to righteousness" (6:19), he does in fact become more and more holy. The unbeliever was getting worse and worse, but under the new Master, the believer is becoming better and better. Second, the end result of this growth in godliness is *eternal life* in the very presence of God. These great benefits are reason enough to submit happily to our good Master.

Paul seals the point with a double contrast. "For the wages of sin is death, but the free gift is eternal life in Christ Jesus our Lord." Which Lord does it benefit to follow? On the one hand, the law requires lifelong conscious effort to be good enough. The moralist pushes hard on the hamster wheel because he is trying to earn a wage. On the other hand, those under grace receive a free gift on the front end before doing any work. Salvation is given, not earned.

Secondly, on the one hand, the payment for all that hard work turns out to be death. What a devastating surprise for the prideful moralist who was looking forward to payday on the Day of Judgment. But on the other hand, the free gift of eternal life transcends Judgment Day. Since the demands of justice were meted out on Passover Day, 33AD, there no longer remains a terrifying expectation of judgment (Hebrews 10:27). Believers won't even need to go before the Great White Throne of God (Revelation 20:11-15). We will stand before Christ's "Bema"—the judgment seat where Christ will address all the acts of a Christian (1 Corinthians 3:10-14)—to receive rewards for our pure service and also to see any impure service burned up as worthless. But we ourselves are already saved. So which Master is it wiser to serve? Which offers benefits? The law offers the wages of breaking the law, which is death. The Lord Jesus offers the free gift of eternal life.

7:1-6   Or do you not know, brethren (for I am speaking to those who know the law), that the law has jurisdiction over a person as long as he lives? For the married woman is bound by law to her husband while he is living; but if her husband dies, she is released from the law concerning her husband. So then, if while her husband is living she is joined to another man, she shall be called an adulteress; but if her husband dies, she is free from the law, so that she is not an adulteress though she is joined to another man. Therefore, my brethren, you also were made to die to the Law through the body of Christ, so that you might be joined to another, to Him who was raised from the dead, in order that we might bear fruit for God. For while we were in the flesh, the sinful passions, which were aroused by the Law, were at work in the members of our body to bear fruit for death. But now we have been released from the Law, having died to that by which we were bound, so that we serve in newness of the Spirit and not in oldness of the letter.

Paul continues to help us as believers to see ourselves as good. He has shown the believer that he or she is on Grace Road instead of Law Road. Grace Road is a beneficial slavery. When God is your Lord, He bestows the kind gifts of sanctification and eternal life upon His servant before the servant does anything. So, the servant goes forth gladly submitting to his Lord because the good news about the Lord has worked a change of heart and mind in the servant. The servant must learn to think properly about himself, seeing himself as dead to sin and alive to righteousness.

Law Road is a dead end. It requires ever-increasing effort but only pays the wage of death. Now the apostle once again helps us think aright by employing an analogy about the relationship between the law and death. We already saw that the law can only bring death, but now we see that the law no longer applies once a person who was under it *dies*. The analogy is important, because it helps us *think* of ourselves as *dead* to the law and therefore *free* in Christ.

Would an IRS agent go to a cemetery to collect unpaid taxes from a man in a grave? It is one thing that the government would seek to tax an estate. That is still a tax against the living. As long as a man is living, taxes are as sure to be owed as surely as death awaits us all. But once a man dies, the law can require nothing from the dead man. He has no fear of being fined. He is not worried about wage garnishment. He hasn't the least concern about going to jail. The law has no power over him, because the law is only in effect among the living.

God tells Christians to think of themselves as being dead to His Law. In Paul's day, a woman who could not stand her husband did not have the option of divorce. Her only hope of living out her days without being bound to him was if he died. If he died, all marriage laws would immediately become irrelevant. She would be free from him.

Paul's analogy becomes complicated because in real life the "husband" to which the illustration corresponds does not die. The Law does not die. Rather it is we who die. And yet the point remains, because in the case of marriage law, it takes two living parties for the law to be in effect. The death of either party in a marriage contract is the end of it.

So, the larger point is that we ought to think of ourselves as having died and been set free from the requirements of the Law. The ritual requirements that govern what an Israelite is allowed to eat, what he is allowed to wear, how he is allowed to dress do not apply to us. Even the ethical requirements cannot demand our death when we break them. They remain instructive to us, showing us the difference between right and wrong in order that we may live to please our new Master. But since we died, the Law cannot demand the penalty of death against us.

We are free from condemnation. We need not live in fear. Our old "husband" is set aside, and we are married to a new One. We are dead to the old quality of life where striving for moral and ritual obedience left us breathless, constantly aware of what failures we were. We are alive to the new quality of life where serving a loving Master who has already and forever accepted us is a pleasure and the desire of our hearts.

The resurrected Christ offers a new way to serve God. It is not a dry begrudging servitude. It is the "newness of the Spirit." The believer naturally bears fruits like love, joy, peace, patience, kindness, goodness, faithfulness, gentleness and self-control (Galatians 5:22-23). Even as an apple tree doesn't have to strain to push out apples, rather they emerge naturally as sap flows within the tree's branches, so also the fruit of the Spirit emerges from believers naturally as the Holy Spirit moves inside the believer. This new life in the Spirit is the crescendo of Paul's argument in this vision of the new you (Romans 6-8). Romans 8 will teach its wonderful truths, but for now, hear it mentioned in contrast to the old way things used to be.

Being under the Law was like being married to a harsh husband and despairing even of life. The believer needs to see that death has in fact set him or her free. Somehow, when Christ died and rose again, God reckoned that the believer, who is identified with Christ, also died and rose with Him. So the demands of Law were left behind, and the believer must now reckon himself or herself as dead to sin, alive in Christ, and forever free from the cruel taskmaster that is the Law.

21

Questions

"for sin, taking an opportunity through the commandment, deceived me and through it killed me"

—Romans 7:11

In this fourth major section of the book of Romans (chapters 6-8), Paul poses and answers questions as his train of thought brings them up. Clearly, he is trying to shape the way a believer thinks. How ought the believer think about himself as he relates to the world, being that he is justified by faith and no longer under the Law? This has been the major question up unto this point. But now, turning the focus directly upon the Law, Paul shapes the way we are to think about it. It is important as you gather a new vision about a new you, no longer under the Law, that you don't turn and condemn the Law itself as being evil.

7:7-12   What shall we say then? Is the Law sin? May it never be! On the contrary, I would not have come to know sin except through the Law; for I would not have known about coveting if the Law had not said, "You shall not covet." But sin, taking opportunity through the commandment, produced in me coveting of every kind; for apart from the Law sin is dead. I was once

> alive apart from the Law; but when the commandment came, sin became alive and I died; and this commandment, which was to result in life, proved to result in death for me; for sin, taking an opportunity through the commandment, deceived me and through it killed me. So then, the Law is holy, and the commandment is holy and righteous and good.

The Law in itself is holy, that is, set apart for God. It is righteous, that is, without sin. It is good, that is, perfectly consistent with God's loving nature. The problem is not the Law, but our sin. The Law is like a wall of stone. We are like fools who run straight into it with the expectation of passing right through. It is harsh in the sense that it has no give. Unlike the stone tablets containing the original Ten Commandments that Moses broke on Mt. Sinai, the Law cannot really be broken. Defy what is written upon those tablets, and you will break yourself against God's Word. The Law is most unyielding. But the lust of the eyes, the lust of the flesh, and especially the pride of life (1 John 2:16) entice sinners to test the fortitude of the Law.

Sin, not the Law, produces coveting in us. The Law exposes covetousness for what it is. Someone who has read the Ten Commandments might conclude that he is not a lawbreaker because he never murdered anyone, never had adulterous contact with anyone, and never took God's name in vain. But coveting is not an outward work. It is an inward thought in the heart of a person. Paul recognizes that since the Law not only outlaws certain outward behaviors but even the inward thoughts and attitudes of the heart, it is far more rigorous than the moralist understands it to be. The moralist judges himself to be okay. But that is only because he is not *really* reading the Law. When a person realizes that the Law condemns all forms of coveting, the Law springs to life in the mind of that person. He realizes in that moment that he is actually a walking dead man.

When inmates on death row make their final walk to the place of execution, there has been a custom whereby the escorting officer shouts, "dead man walking." That is what the Law says to the man who truly considers his ways. If for a moment he is honest about his heart, he will recognize how he broke the law against adultery every time he entertained a lustful thought in his heart. He murdered with hatred in his heart. He made idols whenever his heart put anything in this world ahead of God. When the Law outlaws anything, there is something in the sinner's heart that craves for it, and even more when told that it is forbidden. So sin uses the Law to kill us. As soon as our eyes look intently into the Law, it tells us that we are dead men walking.

7:13   Therefore did that which is good become a cause of death for me? May it never be! Rather it was sin, in order that it would be shown to be sin by effecting death through that which is good, so that through the commandment sin would become utterly sinful.

Our death certificate will not list the Law as our cause of death. Rather it was our own sin that killed us. Sin, being as vile as it is, grabbed hold of a good thing and used it as an instrument to stir up more sin in the life of the sinner. Our sin natures are so utterly sinful that when told not to do something, we are more likely, not less likely, to want to do it. Sin delighted in using the Law to make us worse. But God's purpose of exposing sin in us—to drive us to the loving arms of the Savior—still remains.

22

Conflicted

"I find then the principle that evil is present in me,
the one who wants to do good"

—*Romans 7:21*

Recall from the first section of this book—the overview of The Way to be Good with God (Romans 1:1-17)—that Paul's Christian life serves as a model for us. Paul's self-identification as a slave of Jesus Christ is the destination to which the gospel is taking us. What we see in Paul, the way he glorifies Jesus, the way he loves and prays and strives on mission for the gospel, is what we want for ourselves. But the longer we walk the grace road as a Christian, the more we recognize how far short we are still falling.

Someone has rightly observed that as Christians mature, we repent more even if we sin less. We become more and more aware of our sin, and it frustrates us because we know that we no longer have to sin. Jesus is our ultimate model, and He never sins. But at this point on the Romans Road, it is especially helpful that God gave us Paul to emulate, even as he seeks to emulate Christ (1 Corinthians 11:1). Paul was keenly aware of his own internal struggle between the newness of life that he had in the Spirit and the old sinful nature that we are to learn to reckon as being dead.

Somehow, that old dead dog still bites. We are commanded to consider ourselves dead to sin (Romans 6:11), but that does not mean that moral perfection is possible on this side of heaven, even for the Christian. Since Romans 6-8 poses and answers questions to people who have already received justification through faith (Romans 3:21-5:21), it clearly aims to shape the thinking of the believer. How then are we to think about the continued *presence* of sin in our lives?

7:14-20   For we know that the Law is spiritual, but I am of the flesh, sold into bondage to sin. For what I am doing, I do not understand; for I am not practicing what I would like to do, but I am doing the very thing I hate. But if I do the very thing I do not want to do, I agree with the Law, confessing that the Law is good. So now, no longer am I the one doing it, but sin which dwells in me. For I know that nothing good dwells in me, that is, in my flesh; for the willing is present in me, but the doing of the good is not. For the good that I want, I do not do, but I practice the very evil that I do not want. But if I am doing the very thing I do not want, I am no longer the one doing it, but sin which dwells in me.

Paul's confession in Romans 7:14-20 resonates with what the Apostle John taught. "This is the message we have heard from Him and announce to you, that God is light, and in Him there is no darkness at all. If we say that we have fellowship with Him and yet walk in the darkness, we lie and do not practice the truth; but if we walk in the Light as He Himself is in the Light, we have fellowship with one another, and the blood of Jesus His Son cleanses us from all sin. If we say that we have no sin, we are deceiving ourselves and the truth is not in us. If we confess our sins, He is faithful and righteous to forgive us our sins and to cleanse us from all unrighteousness. If we say that we have not sinned, we make Him a liar and His Word is not in us" (1 John 1:5-10).

We were once sinners who were perfectly at home in this world. Then God revealed His wrath against our sin by giving us a good hard look in the mirror of His Word. Not leaving us there, He also revealed His righteousness and manifested His righteousness upon us, so we can say that an alien righteousness has now overtaken us. We who believe are now "saints" walking in a sinful world to which we do not belong.

But we must also admit the reality that although we are made new, our old sin nature is still with us so long as we sojourn in this place. We should now think of this differently, though. It is like having an alien living inside of us—this time the "alien" of our sin nature. It doesn't belong there, but we must not deny its presence. The penalty for sin has been paid, its power broken. But the presence of sin will not be utterly removed from our lives until we get to heaven. So whenever we see it rear its ugly head, we must do as the Apostle John says in the above passage and confess it to the true Lord of our lives. We must speak humbly in agreement with the Lord every time He shows us that in a certain instance we have obeyed sin. If Jesus is our Lord, He is our only Lord. When our words, thoughts or deeds betray that reality, His blood still avails its power to cleanse us. But our part is to confess.

Paul confesses the presence of sin in his heart. What the actual sins were, we are not told. That is a good thing, because now we are free to imagine. Our imaginations will reveal more about our own hearts than about Paul's. We can thus read Paul's words and ask ourselves in what way they ring true concerning our own lives. Are there sins I have committed that I knew I shouldn't have done but did anyway? They need to be confessed. Are there things I omitted that I knew that I should have done? These sins of omission also need to be confessed. In a sense, it is encouraging to us to recognize that even Paul struggled with the old sin nature. Understanding the struggle is part of what we must gather from the vision of the new you of Romans 6-8.

7:21-24   I find then the principle that evil is present in me, the one who wants to do good. For I joyfully concur with the law of God in the inner man, but I see a different law in the members of my body, waging war against the law of my mind and making me a prisoner of the law of sin which is in my members. Wretched man that I am! Who will set me free from the body of this death?

The struggle between the sinful desires of our flesh and godly desires of our spirit will leave every Christian at some point in their Christian walk feeling like a wretch. We know absolutely that Jesus is Lord and worthy of our wholehearted devotion. We think about His blood shed for us on Mount Calvary, and we shudder. We are fully committed to serving Him and Him alone for all of our days. Then in a moment of weakness when the pressures of life are piling up, when the things of this world have distracted our minds, we experience a temptation and give in to it. Sometimes we hardly put up a fight. When our spirits return to prayer, when God beckons our attention back to Him, we feel miserable. What kind of wretch would neglect so great a salvation! We despise our own behavior. And we know ourselves too weak to guarantee that in the future we will not fall again. So we ask, "Who will set me free from the body of this death?"

It is the longing of the Christian soul for its home. It is the cry of the child of God to be in heaven. It is the cry of the Saint for sanctification to be completed. And it brings us right back to the foot of the cross to the place where we first believed.

There is something beautiful about confession. To be sure, our sins usually result in us missing out on something. When I am distracted by sin, God will use another vessel for some great purpose of His. In another world if I had not been so distracted, perhaps I could have been party to something great. But my reality was sinful in those moments. So God used another "jar of clay" to demonstrate His all-surpassing power (2 Corinthians 4:7-9). But when Christians return to Jesus to confess sin, it reminds us from where our righteousness comes. When God sees us struggle, He values the fight. Dead people don't wrestle with sin (Ephesians 2:1). That we strive so hard to obey Him is honoring to Him. That we come to Him when we fail shows that we know Him to be a compassionate, loving Father. Confession means we trust God's heart. It is a huge part of our journey through the jungle of sin.

23

Victorious

*"But if the Spirit of Him who raised Jesus from the dead dwells in you,
He who raised Christ Jesus from the dead will also give life to
your mortal bodies through His Spirit who dwells in you"*

—Romans 8:11

When a believer gets caught in sin, he or she feels conflicted. The Spirit and the flesh pull the believer in opposite directions. But the believer does not need to be forever torn, as if the two forces were equal in magnitude. Rather, the power of the Holy Spirit is infinite, while the power of the flesh is utterly dependent on deception. When the believer pulls the mask off of sin, its attractiveness is exposed for ugliness, and the temptation is broken. When the believer looks in faith, Jesus Christ gives the victory. Justification came by faith. Victory over the deceptive power of sin also comes by faith.

Faith is the right response to the revelation of truth. It is a gift in at least two ways. First, God reveals truth to undeserving people. Unless God sends the message, then we cannot respond to it. Second, in order to respond to it, we need God to work inside of us. We need Him to soften our hearts, because our consciences are seared as if by a hot iron. But even though faith is a gift of God's grace, there is a sense in which faith is our responsibility. We must make choices to respond to God's grace. "Let no one say when he is tempted, "I am being tempted by God"; for God cannot be tempted by evil, and He Himself does not tempt anyone" (James 1:13). In the same way, when we sin, we must not think that God has failed to offer us enough grace to overcome temptation. Quite the contrary, through Jesus Christ, we have everything we need for life and godliness (2 Peter 1:3).

7:25   Thanks be to God through Jesus Christ our Lord! So then, on the one hand I myself am serving the law of God, but on the other, with my flesh the law of sin.

What a triumphant note to sound the end of Paul's discourse on the presence of sin in the believer's life! There is a victory, and that victory is found through the One who conquered sin on Calvary's hill. Paul does not conclude the thought with his body slouched over and his head drooped between his knees. He finishes with a shout of victory. Despite the struggle that is ours for this time, the penalty and power of sin are broken. There will come a day, not too long for any one of us, when the very presence of sin will forever be erased. But until that day, we can rejoice in the fact that our sins are already forgiven, that going forward we don't have to sin, and that for those inexplicable occasions when we do sin, there is still a stream of cleansing blood flowing from the Savior's side to which we are always free to return. Paul concludes his lament by giving thanks to God for forgiveness, even while acknowledging, although he considers himself dead to sin, that sin will still be right there with him like an alien inside until he dies or the Lord comes back to get him.

8:1-8   Therefore there is now no condemnation for those who are in Christ Jesus. For the law of the Spirit of life in Christ Jesus has set you free from the law of sin and death. For what the Law could not do, weak as it was through the flesh, God did: sending His own Son in the likeness of sinful flesh and as an offering for sin, he condemned sin in the flesh, so that the requirement of the Law might be fulfilled in us, who do not walk according to the flesh but according to the Spirit. For those who are according to the flesh set their minds on the things of the flesh, but those who are according to the Spirit, the things of the Spirit. For the mind set on the flesh is death, but the mind set on the Spirit is life and peace, because the mind set on the flesh is hostile toward God; for it does not subject itself to the law of God, for it is not even able to do so, and those who are in the flesh cannot please God.

Two realities are to be celebrated in this passage. First, there can never be condemnation for those of us who are in Christ Jesus. Thanks be to God through Jesus Christ our Lord, all of our sins have been forgiven. That includes not only the sins of the past, but also of the present and future. A building that is no longer inhabitable may be condemned by city management. Under condemnation, it is set apart for destruction. But we have already been set apart (sanctified) for eternal life. So condemnation is an impossibility. When we sin, we will feel a deep conviction in our hearts that leads us to confession and repentance, but God will not reject us on account of our sin.

Secondly, it is the impartation of the Spirit of God into our lives that designates us (sets us apart) as belonging to God forever. Whereas the Law given through Moses brought condemnation, since the death penalty was attached to the Law, the indwelling presence of the Holy Spirit in our lives will change us from the inside out, conforming us to make us holy, the way He is. This law of the Spirit does affect our morality. Our thoughts, words and deeds are changed, but not through our sheer will power. The Law was weak, because once broken by sinful flesh, it was powerless to save. There were provisions for sinners, sacrifices that needed to be offered. But those were only shadows of the real sacrifice that Jesus made "as an offering for sin." The commandments could do nothing but condemn.

How does the indwelling presence of the Spirit make us holy? He occupies our minds! The things that interest God begin to capture our minds. When all we had were rules to follow, we couldn't get our minds off the things that were forbidden. Of all the trees available to Adam and Eve, why were they even interested in eating from the Tree of the Knowledge of Good and Evil? Since it was forbidden, the law provoked them to think about how it was pleasant to the eyes and also desirable to make them wise (Genesis 3:6). Sin used the law to stir up the mind to acts that led to death. But the Holy Spirit stirs up the mind to acts that lead to life.

"The mind set on the Spirit is life and peace." It is life because the Christian mind thinks about things that will last forever, especially God Himself. It is peace because the Christian mind is right with God. It is not worried about a coming Judgment Day. It is not concerned about performing the right rituals. It is not even stressed about ethical behavior.

The Christian mind is set at ease because the life of the Spirit leads the person to think about spiritual things and please God in thought, word and deed without even straining. It comes naturally as the Holy Spirit does His work in the believer's heart.

Without the Holy Spirit living inside a person, it is impossible for a person to please God. Even when he forces himself to be obedient to the law, the flesh still craves things that are contrary. A religious person may claim to love God, but he is actually hostile toward God since his fleshly mind still thinks about the things that the law says he cannot have.

8:9-11   However, you are not in the flesh but in the Spirit, if indeed the Spirit of God dwells in you. But if anyone does not have the Spirit of Christ, he does not belong to Him. If Christ is in you, though the body is dead because of sin, yet the spirit is alive because of righteousness. But if the Spirit of Him who raised Jesus from the dead dwells in you, He who raised Christ Jesus from the dead will also give life to your mortal bodies through His Spirit who dwells in you.

When we are told that we "are not in the flesh," this does not refer to our good days only. It is not about Christians responding to situations from a spiritual perspective. Likewise, "in the Spirit" does not refer here to being caught up into an ecstasy or to handling a situation in an especially godly way. Rather, "if indeed the Spirit of God dwells in you" refers to the condition of being saved. Either someone has been born again (John 3:3), born of the Spirit, or he has not. As people who have been justified by faith, we are now being taught the reality that the Holy Spirit actually dwells in us. He never leaves.

Because the Holy Spirit indwells Christians, our spirits have been made alive. How so? The Holy Spirit has united with the spirit of the believer, and the spirit that the Holy Spirit touches comes alive. It remains that our bodies will one day die (unless Jesus raptures us before our dying day), but our spirits are alive forevermore. This is why, when Jesus calls Himself the resurrection and the life (John 11:25-26), He says that the one who believes in Him "will never die." The spirit of the man cannot die, and even though the body will, even that will be resurrected. "He who raised Christ Jesus from the dead will also give life to your mortal bodies." This is an added future benefit that corresponds to the present reality that the Holy Spirit has already brought to life the spirit of the believer.

8:12-17   So then, brethren, we are under obligation, not to the flesh, to live according to the flesh—for if you are living according to the flesh, you must die; but if by the Spirit you are putting to death the deeds of the body, you will live. For all who are being led by the Spirit of God, these are sons of God. For you have not received a spirit of slavery leading to fear again, but you have received a spirit of adoption as sons by which we cry out, "Abba! Father!" The Spirit Himself testifies with our spirit that we are children of God, and if children, heirs also, heirs of God and fellow heirs with Christ, if indeed we suffer with Him so that we may also be glorified with Him.

There are only two options presented in this passage. The first, genuine Christianity, is the life of the Spirit. A person who has the Spirit will of necessity be "putting to death the deeds of the body." If he does not feel an obligation to do so, then it is certain that he is still "in the flesh" and the Spirit does not dwell in him.

What else can we who believe in Jesus learn about our new life in union with the Spirit? **First**, the Spirit is leading us toward godliness. We are not alone on this journey. We are being directed step by step. The Christian life is not about effort. Self-help books will do us no good. The key to the Christian life is *yielding*. We must learn to yield our will to the will of the Spirit who now lives inside of us.

Second, we are regarded as sons and daughters of God as we progress in our journey toward Him. We progress in godliness, which is like traveling closer to heaven. Heaven is our home. It is where our Father is. The idea that we are children of God will be a key theme that Paul develops throughout the rest of chapter 8.

Third, since we are adopted sons and daughters, we do not need to be afraid, but can even talk to God like a child calls out for "Daddy." Fear is one of the primary struggles of childhood. Children are vulnerable and dependent, and they know it. But when a child is near her daddy, she is not afraid. She imagines that he can rescue her from anything. In the case of earthly fathers, although we would struggle to the death to protect our children, we cannot absolutely deliver them from all danger. Our Father in heaven can.

Fourth, we will receive an inward confirmation, a deep inexplicable sense in our spirit, that we really are children of God. Since we truly are His kids, He doesn't want us wondering if we are. He will confirm to our hearts that we belong. Our loving Father does not want us doubting that we belong to Him, so He grants to His children an inward assurance of salvation.

Finally, although our journey as pilgrims in this world will require a great struggle against sin, although the world itself will batter us along the way, we should delight that our inheritance is waiting for us in heaven. Suffering, therefore, is only a sign that we are on the right path, never an indication that our Father doesn't care. Having the Holy Spirit inside of us is the source of a tremendous sense of security. Like the child-to-Father relationship theme, the suffering theme will continue through the end of chapter 8.

24

Suffering

*"For I consider that the sufferings of this present
time are not worthy to be compared with the
glory that is to be revealed to us"*

—*Romans 8:18*

The *vision of the new you* would be incomplete if it did not include a
realistic assessment of Christian suffering. "For to you it has been
granted for Christ's sake, not only to believe in Him, but also to suffer for
His sake" (Philippians 1:29). The presence of suffering is not a sign that
the new life is absent, but the opposite is true. Suffering is an important
part of the new life. Along with the gift of eternal life, God allows
suffering to enter our lives, but only to accomplish great purposes.

8:18-25   For I consider that the sufferings of this present time
                 are not worthy to be compared with the glory that is to
                 be revealed to us. For the anxious longing of the
                 creation waits eagerly for the revealing of the sons of
                 God. For the creation was subjected to futility, not
                 willingly, but because of Him who subjected it, in
                 hope that the creation itself also will be set free from
                 its slavery to corruption into the freedom of the glory

of the children of God. For we know that the whole creation groans and suffers the pains of childbirth together until now. And not only this, but also we ourselves groan within ourselves, waiting eagerly for our adoption as sons, the redemption of our body. For in hope we have been saved, but hope that is seen is not hope; for who hopes for what he already sees? But if we hope for what we do not see, with perseverance we wait eagerly for it.

Some environmentalists interpret this passage in such a way as to make it say a lot about the environment, but it is primarily about Christians. We, the children of God, are called to endure suffering for a time in a fallen world. We are here being taught to await eagerly something far better than the broken world in which we live.

The groaning of creation is employed as a metaphor. It is not that trees literally cry when tree harvesters clear another section of the jungle. It is not that animals are panting in the heat because humans have released too much carbon dioxide into the atmosphere. It is not about the sad tears of a polar bear drifting away on an iceberg that has broken loose in the arctic. God made polar bears with the ability to swim.

Rather, it is about brokenness in the world as it affects humans, brokenness that came about as a result of human sin. Had sin not entered the world, there would be no hurricanes, tornados, earthquakes, tsunamis, Ebola viruses, animal attacks or other manifestations of death in the world. The penalty for sin is death, and the entrance of death into the cosmos brought symptoms of death to every corner of the universe. The whole of creation groans metaphorically in that the creation was not designed to be this way. But that it is this way is a reality with which the children of God will have to deal. As long as we are here in this broken world, expect "the sufferings of this present time."

As children of God, we are taught that the sufferings of this world "are not worthy to be compared with the glory that is to be revealed to us." Although we groan in pain as we suffer in a groaning world, God will not leave us here forever. Not only are His children rescued out of this world individually as each of us dies, which for us is only a release from our suffering in a world to which we do not belong, but there is also coming a day when God will create a new heavens and a new earth that are not tainted by sin and death.

Like the Garden of Eden, the new world will have "the freedom of the glory of the children of God." This means that God will receive glory from His new creation, but that glory will come to Him through the children of God. As we enjoy life in His presence in the environment that He has created for us to live in, we will be satisfied. It won't matter how beautiful the creation is, how much there is to do, or how exciting it is— although the pattern of the Garden of Eden would indicate that the new creation will be beautiful, purposeful and exciting. What really matters is that even as God walked with Adam and Eve in the cool of the day (Genesis 3:8), God will walk with us. We will be satisfied because we will be with God, and He will be glorified in the way in which we walk with Him.

Walking with God is the point of our current text. The point is that we do not have to wait until God makes everything new in order to walk with Him. He wants us to be joyful now in our knowledge of what is coming later. We don't yet have the "redemption of our body," meaning resurrected bodies fit for the new heaven and new earth. But having the hope of this, we are able to persevere in the midst of suffering. We are the children of God who "walk . . . according to the Spirit" (Romans 8:4), who are being "led by the Spirit of God" (8:14). So our walk with Him has already begun. He will go with us no matter what suffering comes our way. We can persevere knowing that it is only for a very short time compared to the eternity we have waiting for us in the world He is preparing for us. As we walk with the Spirit, even now, He helps us focus on our hope rather than our present sufferings.

8:26-27   In the same way the Spirit also helps our weakness; for we do not know how to pray as we should, but the Spirit Himself intercedes for us with groanings too deep for words; and He who searches the hearts knows what the mind of the Spirit is, because He intercedes for the saints according to the will of God.

Walking with the Spirit directs our hope to heaven (8:18-25) and helps us pray for God's will to be done on earth as it is in heaven (8:26-27). The Holy Spirit lives inside us and from that location communicates with the Father and the Son. The things that are discussed in that dialogue within the Trinity are too deep for words. But since we walk in the Spirit, His intercession rubs off on us. We learn to pray like Him.

Our flesh is so weak, so damaged by the fall, that we do not naturally pray. One would think that a created being would always long to be in communication with his Creator. We should, in fact, pray unceasingly. Remember Paul's unceasing prayer life that he models for us in Romans 1:8-13? We must learn to pray like that, "to pray as we should" (8:26). The longer and closer we walk with the Spirit, the more we pray like Him.

As we learn, it is comforting for children like us to know that as the Father looks into our hearts, He always sees the Holy Spirit there praying. Even when we don't pray as we should, the Spirit is always asking the will of God to be done in our lives. Because of this intercession, the perfect intercession from God to God, we know that His prayers will be answered. The will of God *will* be done in our lives.

25

Purpose

*"And we know that God causes all things to work together
for good to those who love God, to those who are called
according to His purpose"*

—Romans 8:28

The bad things that happen in this world, the sources of our suffering,
are not God's ultimate will. His ultimate will is for Himself to be
glorified in us and for us to be satisfied in Him. However, God does *allow*
everything that happens to us. From our vantage point, especially when we
are in the midst of suffering, it is very difficult for us to see how God's
ultimate will is going to be done. But we have already learned that even
when our spirits are not as prayerful as they should be, the Holy Spirit is
united with our Spirit and is constantly interceding for the will of God to
be done. We know His prayers are always answered, so we need to trust
God no matter what happens to us on earth.

8:28-30   And we know that God causes all things to work
together for good to those who love God, to those who
are called according to His purpose. For those whom
He foreknew, He also predestined to become
conformed to the image of His Son, so that He would

> be the firstborn among many brethren; and these whom He predestined, He also called; and these whom He called, He also justified; and these whom He justified, He also glorified.

God is not the ultimate *cause* of suffering. Sin, taking opportunity from the Law, has deceived us and produced in us every kind of covetous desire. Sin, by the Law, put us to death. So, we only have human *sin* to blame for all the symptoms of death we see in the world.

God is the *cause* of how everything that happens to His children will work together for the good of the child. We were "called according to His purpose." So there will be a purpose for anything that happens to us. The thing itself may not be good. But like a doctor with an instrument performing a surgery, God will use everything, painful things included, to change us in ways for which we will be eternally grateful.

We, the children of God, are the objects of His love. God is accomplishing something in us, something that nothing can stop. Each of us is being made to be *like Jesus*. We are being reshaped. As we walk with God, the Holy Spirit works in our lives to accomplish this transformation. We are sons and daughters. He did not save us and adopt us into His family with the intent of keeping us as we are. Our thoughts, words, and deeds were ugly on account of our sin nature that we inherited from Adam. But Jesus, the Second Adam, the sinless Son, is the perfect representative of what God intended human beings to be.

Through what has been called the Golden Chain of Redemption, God is absolutely accomplishing this transformation in us. All things work together toward this end, suffering included. But the end result is certain, since the chain cannot be broken. It began before the world began when God, who knows everything, already knew everything about us, especially that we would be among His children.

As certainly as He knew us, He predestined everything in our lives to happen exactly as they do. Having predestined everything that would serve to make us like Jesus, it follows that this included the moment when hearing the gospel, our hearts would be called to believe. Believing ones were sure to be justified. Justified ones were sure to be glorified, which brings us back around to the final condition of the one who is being conformed into the image of Jesus. Jesus, the Glory of the Father, is the One into whose likeness we are being transformed. Children of God, who have the inward testimony of the Spirit that we are indeed children, can rest assured that no matter what befalls us, it works for our good in making us like Jesus.

8:31-36   What then shall we say to these things? If God is for us, who is against us? He who did not spare His own Son, but delivered Him over for us all, how will He not also with Him freely give us all things? Who will bring a charge against God's elect? God is the one who justifies; who is the one who condemns? Christ Jesus is He who died, yes, rather who was raised, who is at the right hand of God, who also intercedes for us. Who will separate us from the love of Christ? Will tribulation, or distress, or persecution, or famine, or nakedness, or peril, or sword? Just as it is written, "FOR YOUR SAKE WE ARE BEING PUT TO DEATH ALL DAY LONG; WE WERE CONSIDERED AS SHEEP TO BE SLAUGHTERED."

The story of our lives is suffering all day long. There are times of prosperity. There are times of rest and relaxation. There are weddings, births, and birthdays, and thousands of blessings in the course of a Christian life. These times are especially pronounced in the United States of America, a country founded on the principles of the Bible. But the missionary who leaves the U.S. for a place like Syria may soon feel like a sheep to be slaughtered. The reality is that even in the U.S., the more closely a Christian holds to the worldview of the Bible, the more he will see the culture at large as a place of suffering. The more he preaches the Word of God, the more he will suffer persecution. Hopefully it will not come to slaughter in the U.S., but it has already come to ridicule.

The Christian does not identify himself as a victim. He does not slump his shoulders and frown at the world. He is the most joyful man on the planet because he knows the answers to the questions that matter more than suffering.

"What then shall we say to these things?" Our Father is making us like His Son, so we are willing to accept pain.

"If God is for us, who is against us?" Everyone in the world can rally against us, but all of their power is nothing compared to God's.

"He who did not spare His own Son, but delivered Him over for us all, how will He not also with Him freely give us all things?" God may lead us through the fire, but the gift of Jesus dying for us on the cross has erased any question as to whether He loves us, so we know that the fire is only for our refining.

"Who will bring a charge against God's elect?" The world will charge us with narrow-mindedness, intolerance, racism, bigotry, and any insult they can fashion, but if the Judge sees things differently, then let them holler what they want.

"God is the one who justifies; who is the one who condemns?" God has already pronounced us justified on account of our faith in the blood of His Son, so these accusers are like petulant children in our eyes.

"Christ Jesus is He who died, yes, rather who was raised, who is at the right hand of God, who also intercedes for us. Who will separate us from the love of Christ?" His love endures forever.

"Will tribulation, or distress, or persecution, or famine, or nakedness, or peril, or sword?" Come what may, we will not be moved. We walk in the Spirit and God works everything together for our good.

8:37-39   But in all these things we overwhelmingly conquer through Him who loved us. For I am convinced that neither death, nor life, nor angels, nor principalities, nor things present, nor things to come, nor powers, nor height, nor depth, nor any other created thing, will be able to separate us from the love of God, which is in Christ Jesus our Lord.

Brothers and sisters in Christ, it is time for us to look intently into the perfect law that gives liberty. It is time to understand the law of the Spirit. When we walk by the Spirit, we experience life to the fullest. It is time for us to see the vision of the *new you* that Romans 6-8 provides.

We see the world differently when the scales are lifted from our eyes and we behold the glory that is in the face of Jesus Christ (2 Corinthians 4:4-6). Having heard the Word, in the instant we believe (Ephesians 1:13), we are justified by faith and the Holy Spirit comes to live inside of us. He conforms us into the image of Jesus. So, we must continually reckon ourselves dead to sin and alive to Christ (Romans 6:11). We must recognize the futility of striving to obey the rituals and ethics of the law and instead live by the Spirit (7:4). We must not allow discouragement to take over when we see sin in our lives (7:24), but instead must learn to walk by the Spirit (8:2). We must yield to Him (8:4), accept His inward testimony that we are God's children (8:16), and pray in accordance with the groanings He awakens in us (8:26). We must walk boldly in the world (8:18), not afraid of the sufferings that will come (8:36), but confident in the love of the Father (8:37-39).

This confident stance in the love of the Father is the place where Paul leaves us. We are still in the jungle of sin, aware of the pain of thorns, aware of the bite of serpents who poke at the old man inside of us, striving to bring it back to life. But we have the Holy Spirit living inside of us, and we are loved! So we walk with the expectation of overwhelmingly conquering anything that opposes the knowledge of God and the gospel of our Lord Jesus Christ. If that great serpent of old, the devil himself, should oppose us, then in Christ we will do as the first Adam should have. We will stomp on his head.

Should the world subject us to suffering, even to beheading at the sword, we will accept it joyfully in the knowledge of what awaits us. Nothing can separate us from the love of God that is in Christ Jesus. We are the children of God, made holy by the Spirit, victorious in the jungle of sin. When you believe in Jesus, you are justified by faith, so gaze intently at this vision of the *new you*.

SECTION 5

Good God Almighty
Behind the Scenes
Romans 9-11

26

Compassion

"For I could wish that I myself were accursed, separated
from Christ for the sake of my brethren, my kinsmen
according to the flesh"

—Romans 9:3

If you have received the teaching thus far (Romans 1-8), then you know that you are secure, even though you are still standing in the jungle of sin. Before the gospel came to you, you were a dead man walking. The jungle was inescapable, but you still thought that you were okay. By God's grace, even while you were a self-deluded sinner, the gospel came to you and opened your eyes to the truth. You took a good hard look in the mirror of God's law (1:18-3:20) and became aware of your true condition. Then a manifestation of God's righteousness (3:21-5:21) justified you when you placed your trust in Jesus. As your eyes adjusted to a vision of a new you (6-8), you began to reckon yourself dead to sin and alive in Christ. You realized that God's Holy Spirit indwells you. So now you see yourself as a child of God who stands secure in His love, whatever may come your way.

Still, your heavenly Father is not yet ready to have you go anywhere. In this next section of Romans 9-11, He rolls away the distracting canopy of the trees of this world. Turning your eyes up to heaven, He opens up the clouds of the sky like a scroll. He gives you a glimpse behind the scenes.

This is not so much a vision of heaven. He unveils heaven at the end of the last book of the Bible (Revelation 21-22). It is, rather, a glimpse of how God is sovereign over history. As time progresses, as all the events of this world unfold, God is at work behind the scenes. His providence over history extends from the micro to the macro. He is intimately involved with the very hearts of every individual who has ever lived, while at the same time He directs the course of nations.

It is fitting that the book of Romans would include this section. The gospel is a message for individual sinners. It tells us the way to be saved. But the gospel is first of all a message about God, not a message about man. We are the joyful recipients of God's grace. But the God of grace is the author of the gospel that saves us. The good news brings glory to Almighty God, especially for His goodness.

At the end of Romans 8, we stand triumphant over the things of this world. We are adopted children of God. We are forever secure in His love. But we look out upon the world, and we see that not everyone is standing with us. The most startling among those who refuse the gospel, those who are therefore still lost, are a majority of the Jewish people. Many of "the children of God" (Deuteronomy 14:1) are not among "the children of God" (Romans 8:16)! The fact that many people will be eternally lost, even so many of the Jewish people, is a sad reality that must be addressed.

We will be sent out to live among the people of the world and to preach the gospel wherever we go. Practical instructions for how to conduct ourselves as we go will comprise the tail end of the book of Romans (chapters 12-16). But before we go, we must see a glimpse behind the scenes. Unless we recognize who controls history, even the course of human hearts, then our mission will be too much for us to bear.

9:1-5   I am telling the truth in Christ, I am not lying, my conscience testifies with me in the Holy Spirit, that I have great sorrow and unceasing grief in my heart. For I could wish that I myself were accursed, separated from Christ for the sake of my brethren, my kinsmen according to the flesh, who are Israelites, to whom belongs the adoption as sons, and the glory and the covenants and the giving of the Law and the temple service and the promises, whose are the fathers, and

from whom is the Christ according to the flesh, who is
over all, God blessed forever. Amen.

Paul is nearly crushed by the weight of his burden for his Jewish
countrymen. Were it not for his full confidence in Christ, who is
completely sovereign "over all," Paul would have been overcome by grief.
That Paul emotes so sorrowfully here at the beginning of a new section of
his letter to the Romans is particularly striking given the exultant, even
jubilant note with which he ended the last section. It is likely that as Paul
delighted in the love of God and finished expressing it in writing, the Holy
Spirit struck Paul with a sobering reminder that not everyone is currently
enjoying the same love.

Paul's letter to the Philippians is another Scripture that will help us
understand the shift of Paul's emotion here at the start of this section. Like
Romans 9, the book of Philippians reveals how completely Jewish Paul
was (Philippians 3:1-6). But Paul's identification with Christ so utterly
trumped his identification as a Jew that he considered the latter as rubbish
compared to "the surpassing value of knowing Christ Jesus my Lord"
(Philippians 3:8).

It wasn't that Paul ceased being Jewish. Neither was it true that
Paul stopped loving his Jewish people. Rather, the case was that Paul
loved Christ so much that even if the entire nation of Israel rejected their
Messiah, then Paul was willing to be rejected with Him. By and large, the
Israelites were rejecting Christ. As Christ's ambassador, Paul was also
being rejected. Wherever Paul went throughout the Roman Empire, the
first place he stopped in any given city was the Jewish Synagogue. All day
long, he held out his hand to them. The book of Philippians ends up
placing an emphasis upon *joy* because the greatness of Christ (Philippians
2:9-11) is so absolute that even the lostness of men, even the lostness of
much of Israel, will not ultimately dampen that joy.

In Romans 9, Paul demonstrates that joy and sorrow can coexist in
the heart of the Christian. His sorrow is a model of Christian compassion.
In his wish that he shares with us in the above passage, Paul demonstrates
a love for the lost that is hard to imagine. Since we know that Paul is not
lying, we must conclude that he is a spiritual giant. As Moses was willing
to have his name blotted out in place of the Israelites (a willingness of
which God approved but did not grant in Exodus 32:32-33), as Jesus was
willing to die in the place of sinners (a willingness He expressed in the
Garden of Gethsemane that God did grant, once and for all in Luke 22:42),
so also Paul was willing to suffer the judgment of God in the place of the
Israelites. Since Jesus alone satisfied the will of the Father by suffering in

the sinners' stead, Paul's request is impossible. But it is nevertheless a model of the kind of love that pleases God. Such love for the brother may seem unthinkable to ordinary Christians. It is, nevertheless, the self-giving love (ἀγάπη, agapé) that we should desire to be formed in us.

27

Election

*"for though the twins were not yet born and had not done anything
good or bad, so that God's purpose according to His choice would
stand, not because of works but because of Him who calls, it was
said to her, 'The older will serve the younger'"*

—*Romans 9:11-12*

Paul expressed his sorrow about the doom of most Israelites by
reflecting upon the covenant and all the special promises that God
originally gave to Israel (9:1-5). But in light of what God promised, does
the unbelief of most Jews mean that God was too weak to bring about the
things He promised?

9:6-13   But it is not as though the word of God has failed. For
          they are not all Israel who are descended from Israel;
          nor are they all children because they are Abraham's
          descendants, but: "THROUGH ISAAC YOUR
          DESCENDANTS WILL BE NAMED." That is, it is
          not the children of the flesh who are children of God,
          but the children of the promise are regarded as
          descendants. For this is the word of promise: "AT
          THIS TIME I WILL COME, AND SARAH SHALL

HAVE A SON." And not only this, but there was Rebekah also, when she had conceived twins by one man, our father Isaac; for though the twins were not yet born and had not yet done anything good or bad, so that God's purpose according to His choice would stand, not because of works but because of Him who calls, it was said to her, "THE OLDER WILL SERVE THE YOUNGER." Just as it is written, "JACOB I LOVED, BUT ESAU I HATED".

It is important here to remember the larger context of Paul's train of thought. What does it say about the validity of the gospel when most Jews rejected the message? After all, Paul couched his message as a fulfillment of the Hebrew Bible. Do you recall the first thing that Paul said about the gospel in his letter to the Romans? He said that the gospel was "promised beforehand" (Romans 1:2) in the Hebrew Scriptures. If most Jews, especially the religious elite, the ones who ought to know the Scriptures best, are not convinced by Paul's arguments, then why would an ordinary Jew, or a Gentile for that matter, believe that the crucified Jesus of Nazareth was actually the Messiah?

Paul actually knew the Hebrew Bible better than those who rejected the Christ. On a human level in his youth, Saul of Tarsus was trained under Gamaliel and proved himself more zealous for the Law than any of his contemporaries (Philippians 3:1-5, Galatians 1:13-14, Acts 8:1-3, 9:1-3, 22:3). On a spiritual level after his conversion, Paul's letters defined Christian orthodoxy and shaped Western culture perhaps more than any man other than Jesus himself.

Paul was convinced that Jesus of Nazareth was the Messiah promised by the prophets of old, and he also found in the prophets the reason why most of the Jews who were his own contemporaries were rejecting the Christ. Paul's claim that Jesus fulfilled the Messianic prophecies (Romans 1:2) was true, and knowing that Israel's national rejection of Christ reflected badly upon the message of Christ, Paul knew that he needed to show the Scriptural context that makes sense of so much rejection.

While Jewish people thought that the world was made up of two classes of people—Jew and Gentile, descendants of Abraham and those who weren't—the truth was different than what they understood. Not all physical descendants of Abraham were truly right with God, and not all Gentiles were truly cut off from God. With regard to the Israelites, within the nation there were two groups in God's eyes. There were the true believers, and there were false pretenders.

This was revealed in the way that God brought forth the nation. Abraham actually had two sons, which typify the two kinds of Israelites. Ishmael represents the "children of the flesh." He was a "wild donkey of a man" (Genesis 16:12) even though he was physically an offspring of Abraham. Isaac represents the "children of the promise." Although Isaac was just as wild and unruly as Ishmael, he was chosen to be a patriarch of the nation of Israel. So the contrast is between the chosen and the not chosen. Although every descendant of Jacob is an Israelite by birth, only the "children of promise" within the nation were truly chosen to belong to God.

The unbelieving are not only typified by Ishmael, but also by Esau. This principle was clearly important to God, so He illustrated it with two living examples. The child of promise—Isaac—also had two sons. One would be like his father—a child of promise. The other would be only a child of the flesh. The story of Jacob and Esau, brothers who share the same heritage but opposite destinies brings the most profound distinction into crystal clear focus. The difference between them is *not* their worthiness, but only God's choice!

God chose for Jacob to be a "child of the promise" before Jacob was born. He passed over the first-born Esau before Esau was even born. So bringing the illustration back around to the point of the passage (9:6-13), it has become clear that the fact that most of the nation of Israel rejects Jesus Christ is no indication that God's Word has failed. Rather, it is just as it has been from the beginning. God has a nation called Israel, but many or most of its citizens are really only Ishmael and Esau, children of the flesh. Those who do believe in Jesus Christ are like Isaac and Jacob. Before they were born, before having done anything good or bad, God chose these Jews to be children of the promise. God blessed them by choosing them ahead of time to be the true believers within His special nation.

28

Mercy

"So then it does not depend on the man who wills or the man who runs, but on God who has mercy"

—Romans 9:16

Paul is not ignorant of the implications of his teaching that God chooses some people to belong to him as his children and passes over others. Paul's natural human reasoning would bristle at the thought just as much as our human reasoning does. If someone is not chosen, then does he not have the right to claim that an injustice was done against him? How is it fair for God to choose one over against another?

9:14-18   What shall we say then? There is no injustice with God, is there? May it never be! For He says to Moses, "I WILL HAVE MERCY ON WHOM I HAVE MERCY, AND I WILL HAVE COMPASSION ON WHOM I HAVE COMPASSION." So then it does not depend on the man who wills or the man who runs, but on God who has mercy. For the Scripture says to Pharaoh, "FOR THIS VERY PURPOSE I RAISED YOU UP, TO DEMONSTRATE MY POWER IN YOU, AND THAT MY NAME BE PROCLAIMED

THROUGHOUT THE WHOLE EARTH." So then He
has mercy on whom He desires, and He hardens whom
He desires.

Paul once again employs the strongest Greek term of negation (μή,
mé) to rule out the possibility that God is unjust. There is no injustice with
God when He judges anyone, "for we have already charged that both Jews
and Greeks are all under sin" (Romans 3:9). Any individual who wants
God's justice is actually asking to die, "for the wages of sin is death"
(Romans 6:23). If God were to allow the whole lot of the human race to
die and depart from Him forever, then He would remain perfectly just.
Therefore, the issue is really one of mercy.

Paul quotes from God's Word to Moses because the larger
question has to do with unbelieving Jewish people. Why are there so many
Jews who do not accept their Messiah? Is it any wonder, considering how
almost universally they rejected God's prophet Moses, the one who served
as a type of Christ? An entire generation of Israelites wandered for forty
years and died off in the wilderness because they were only children of
flesh, not children of promise. Many of their physical children were
children of promise, but the precedent set in Israel is one of unbelief, not
faith! Therefore God is absolutely just, and even the very existence of
Israel confirms His Word, "I will have mercy on whom I have mercy, and
I will have compassion on whom I have compassion." God is free to
bestow mercy and compassion on whomever He pleases, and those who do
not receive it, do by definition receive what they deserve.

9:19-24   You will say to me then, "Why does He still find
                 fault? For who resists His will?" On the contrary, who
                 are you, O man, who answers back to God? The thing
                 molded will not say to the molder, "Why did you make
                 me like this," will it? Or does not the potter have a
                 right over the clay, to make from the same lump one
                 vessel for honorable use and another for common use?
                 What if God, although willing to demonstrate His
                 wrath and to make His power known, endured with
                 much patience vessels of wrath prepared for
                 destruction? And He did so to make known the riches
                 of His glory upon vessels of mercy, which He
                 prepared beforehand for glory, even us, whom He also
                 called, not from among Jews only, but also from
                 among Gentiles.

The charge of injustice in God has already been answered. But that does not mean that children of the flesh will be satisfied with the answer. After all, how common is it for people to receive what they deserve and yet blame others for their condition? It may not appear *fair* to people who are not among the chosen, but every individual who complains about God's fairness is individually guilty of sin. What they say they want to know is why God decides to be merciful to others but not to themselves. But they really don't believe these things anyway. So when they question God's right to judge them, they are actually rejecting God's bad news about the human condition and His good news about the Christ. To blame "God's will" for their rejection is to shift the focus off of the sinner who rejects the gospel, a good news that even now is available to every sinner, should they only accept it.

At this point, God expresses His sovereignty by *ceasing* to answer the objections of the unbeliever. God is free to be merciful. But mercy, by definition, cannot be demanded. The proper position of the penitent is that of a beggar. One ought to beg for mercy, not blame the one who decides whether or not He will give it. The analogy of the potter having freedom over the clay serves to illustrate the truth that sinners in the hands of an angry God have no right to demand anything from Him. The gospel is a call to heart-felt repentance. It promises to make a man new, to make him a vessel for honorable use. But it calls a man to faith, which includes a profound recognition of a need for mercy.

In order to become "a vessel for honorable use," one must first of all be "a vessel of mercy." That is to say, the prideful man who does not beg for mercy, especially after seeing his reflection in the mirror of God's Word (Romans 1:18-3:20), is revealing the perfect justice of the God who leaves him as "a vessel of wrath." Such stubborn pride ought to be punished with immediate death and eternal hell, but God patiently endures the mocking and the scorn of these who spurn His offer of grace expressed in the gospel. When we who believe the gospel see how much time and how many chances God gives to the unbeliever, we become all the more convinced that it was nothing but the great mercifulness of God's character that accounts for our having been made vessels for honorable use.

Why are we vessels of mercy? We see others who, it appears to us, are not. This makes us all the more thankful to God for His mercy because we recognize that "but for the grace of God, there go I." In the end, we have to come back to the thing that had us basking in the love of God after seeing His vision of us (Romans 6-8). We cannot find anything in ourselves that commended us to God, any more than Isaac was better than

Ishmael or Jacob than Esau. Rather, we owe everything to His grace. Paul points us back to the Golden Chain of Redemption.

We are vessels of mercy because God called us to Himself. The gospel did not originate with us. God sent it to us. Our hearts were not predisposed to believe the content of His message, especially since it did not esteem our works whatsoever. God's Spirit drew our hearts. We were called by His Word and His Spirit, and that is the end of the story. We contributed nothing. "For those whom He foreknew, He also predestined to become conformed to the image of His Son, so that He would be the firstborn among many brethren; and these whom He predestined, He also called; and these whom He called, He also justified; and these whom He justified, He also glorified" (Romans 8:29-30). He did it all.

9:25-26   As He says also in Hosea, "I WILL CALL THOSE WHO WERE NOT MY PEOPLE, 'MY PEOPLE,' AND HER WHO WAS NOT BELOVED, 'BELOVED.'" "AND IT SHALL BE THAT IN THE PLACE WHERE IT WAS SAID TO THEM, 'YOU ARE NOT MY PEOPLE,' THERE THEY SHALL BE CALLED SONS OF THE LIVING GOD."

Paul's quotations from Hosea serve to drive home the point that the mercy of God accounts for our salvation, and certainly *not* anything in ourselves. The prophet Hosea had a wife who became a prostitute. As a symbol of God's love for Israel, He commanded Hosea to go to the market and buy her back to himself. The Golden Chain of Redemption was thus illustrated. Hosea chose her to be his wife, called her home, forgave her, and gave her all the rights of an ever-faithful wife. Hosea saved her by paying her debt. This redemption was analogous to how God redeemed Israel.

God's redemption was, in fact, infinitely greater than the earthly example He gave us. It included Gentiles—"but also from among Gentiles" (9:24)—as well as Jews. It forgave an even greater offense (1:18-3:20). It declared us righteous in a more complete and real sense (3:21-5:21). It even made us holy, truly bearing the image of the Son into whose likeness the Spirit actually conforms us (6-8). The analogy is there in the story. We are like Gomer, and Hosea represents God, but the reality is infinitely greater than the analogy.

Hosea had children of flesh. Hosea was instructed to name his daughter "Lo-ruhamah" (Hosea 1:6), which meant, "she has not obtained compassion." Hosea was told to name his son Lo-ammi (Hosea 1:9), meaning "not my people." But the prophet foretold (Hosea 1:10-11) that even among the children of the flesh, there was coming a day for Israel when God would call some to believe in Jesus Christ and thus become His people. These would be those who receive compassion. "I will have compassion on whom I have compassion" (9:15). These would be those that He changes into vessels for honorable use, "even us, whom He also called" (9:24).

God has compassion on us, calls us to Himself, calls us His children, and all this in the midst of the vessels of wrath. "You prepare a table before me in the presence of my enemies" (Psalm 23:5). He has compassion on one and not upon another. He calls one group His children and the other "not my people." God is no different today in electing some to be saved and passing over others than He was in the days of Hosea. But the point that like Gomer all of us were sold into slavery to sin must set the context for understanding that everything we have is only because of mercy.

29

Remnant

"Isaiah cries out concerning Israel, 'Though the number of the sons of Israel be like the sand of the sea, it is the remnant that will be saved"

—Romans 9:27

Paul used two examples (Ishmael and Esau) to illustrate that some Israelites are only Israelites in flesh only (Romans 9:6-13). They are not "children of promise." Now Paul employs a second example from the Old Testament to illustrate that children of flesh are destined for wrath, and our escape from wrath is only owed to compassion and mercy. The first example was the harsh naming of the children of Hosea. The second is the blunt assertion that only a remnant will be spared from coming wrath upon the sons of Israel. A majority, only the remnant excepted, will experience a judgment that rivals what Sodom and Gomorrah received.

9:27-29   Isaiah cries out concerning Israel, "THOUGH THE NUMBER OF THE SONS OF ISRAEL BE LIKE THE SAND OF THE SEA, IT IS THE REMNANT THAT WILL BE SAVED; FOR THE LORD WILL EXECUTE HIS WORD ON THE EARTH, THOROUGHLY AND QUICKLY." And just as

Isaiah foretold, "UNLESS THE LORD OF SABAOTH HAD LEFT TO US A POSTERITY, WE WOULD HAVE BECOME LIKE SODOM, AND WOULD HAVE RESEMBLED GOMORRAH."

Paul is rising to a monumental challenge. The veracity of the gospel is predicated upon the Old Testament prophets of Israel (Romans 1:2), but a majority of Israelites contemporary to Paul were not believing the gospel. What could account for such dissonance? "On the evidence of two witnesses or three witnesses, he who is to die shall be put to death" (Deuteronomy 17:6a). Paul wishes to put the arguments of anti-gospel Jews and Gentiles to death. So, he calls Isaac and Jacob to testify that not everyone who has been called "brother" is really a "child of promise" (Romans 9:6-13). Then Paul calls his star witness—Moses—to testify that God has reserved His sovereign freedom to discriminate, to have mercy upon only the ones whom He desires. Moses heard God say, "I WILL HAVE MERCY ON WHOM I HAVE MERCY, AND I WILL HAVE COMPASSION ON WHOM I HAVE COMPASSION" (Romans 9:15).

Finally, Paul calls Hosea and Isaiah to testify that many Israelites are "not my people" and are therefore destined for wrath, but a remnant among them will be saved (Romans 9:25-29). Isaiah speaks as a last witness, probably because there is no mincing of words in what he has to say. Paul is not ashamed of the gospel (Romans 1:16), and the number of Jews who reject Jesus as their Christ does not move Paul one bit.

As Isaiah gives witness, the utter destruction of Sodom and Gomorrah is typical of the kind of fate that awaits sinners. Unbelievers have no complaint to levy against God if He chooses to judge them right where they are. They have no appeal to justice, no appeal to fairness, and no hope of earning God's salvation by obeying the Law of Moses. "It does not depend on the man who wills or the man who runs, but on God who has mercy" (9:16). Moses and all the prophets experienced the rejection of Israel, by and large, and they foretold the same national rejection that was occurring in Paul's day. It was actually according to God's Word that Israel was rejecting the Christ. God's Word had not failed at all (9:6).

9:30-33   What shall we say then? That Gentiles, who did not pursue righteousness, attained righteousness, even the righteousness which is by faith; but Israel, pursuing a law of righteousness, did not arrive at that law. Why? Because they did not pursue it by faith, but as though it were by works. They stumbled over the stumbling stone, just as it is written, "BEHOLD, I LAY IN ZION A STONE OF STUMBLING AND A ROCK OF OFFENSE, AND HE WHO BELIEVES IN HIM WILL NOT BE DISAPPOINTED."

Paul now returns to his primary identity as the apostle to the Gentiles. Paul expressed gut-wrenching heartbreak to initiate this discussion (9:1-5). Then he explained that there is a remnant of Jews who are being saved in the midst of a national rejection. This rejection will be punished by fire (9:6-29). In Romans 9:30-33, Paul transitions to the Gentiles. Paul always went to the Jews first. He made it his full-time job to preach to the Jews of Corinth, which showed how much he really cared. "But when they resisted and blasphemed, he shook out his garments and said to them, 'Your blood be on your own heads! I am clean. From now on I will go to the Gentiles'" (Acts 18:6).

There were a chosen few—the children of promise—that God knew He would save out of Israel. These were secure in His love because a Golden Chain of Redemption had made their identity as children of God to be an unbreakable certainty. God also knew that a majority of Israel would reject Christ. Since this rejection was not only Paul's experience but also foretold by the prophets, Paul accepted that most Israelites were vessels prepared for destruction. This knowledge broke Paul's heart and caused such sorrow that Paul would have substituted himself in their place and born their punishment in hell. But Paul did not know if any individual Israelite was a vessel of mercy or a vessel of wrath. Only God knew that. So, Paul always extended a heart-felt offer to everyone, Jew and Gentile alike.

Paul knew from Isaiah 28:6 that most Jews would stumble over Jesus Christ. He also anticipated a massive acceptance among the Gentiles. His anticipation certainly played out in history as even the Roman Empire itself would one day call itself "Holy." During the course of nearly two thousand years of church history, billions of Gentiles would believe. Still today, the gospel is advancing beyond Jerusalem and gaining adherents in the farthest places on earth, but in the reestablished nation of Israel, the vast majority of Jews do not believe.

30

Passion

"Brethren, my heart's desire and my prayer to
God for them is for their salvation"

—Romans 10:1

Paul takes no delight in anyone being lost. In chapter nine, he gave us a glimpse behind the scenes of heaven. What happened in the spiritual world that affected the realities we see with our eyes? Specifically, why do we see so many Israelites rejecting the gospel? The answer was that God chooses to be compassionate and merciful to some people by bringing them to salvation, while at the same time, He leaves others in their hardness of heart.

God is perfectly just in His choice to extend mercy (none of us deserve it), but that so many Jews are among those whom He passes over is certainly not an indication that God's Word has failed. In point of fact, the prophets (including Moses, Hosea, and Isaiah) foretold that this would be the case. The Israelites' own stumbling over the Rock of offense was to blame. But God is nevertheless behind the scenes. He brings about His will even in a world where humans rebel against Him. In the past before He created, He elected those whom He would save. Paul knows that most Israelites are not children of promise and on account of their own stubborn fleshly hearts will reject the gospel. But his "heart's desire" for any and every Israelite that He meets is for them to come to repentance and faith in Jesus Christ.

10:1-4   Brethren, my heart's desire and my prayer to God for them is for their salvation. For I testify about them that they have a zeal for God, but not in accordance with knowledge. For not knowing about God's righteousness and seeking to establish their own, they did not subject themselves to the righteousness of God. For Christ is the end of the law for righteousness to everyone who believes.

Notice that the salvation of Jews is Paul's "prayer to God for them." This is crucial to notice, because Paul's knowledge of God's sovereignty does not preclude Paul from asking God to accomplish what Paul most desires. Paul is clearly submitted to God's will for Israel, which includes what the prophets foretold about national rejection, but he asks God to be willing to save Jewish people. As we saw in the overview (Romans 1:1-17), a person who has arrived at God's destination—alive in Christ, walking in the Spirit—is a person who prays unceasingly. His prayers are celebratory and thankful, but also largely comprised of supplication. To supplicate is to ask God for things, even to cry out like a beggar.

The point of praying for God to save Israelites is that it is, in fact, God who saves. One might look at the teaching of Romans 9 from a cynical angle and conclude that since God is sovereign even over the hearts of men, there is no point in trying to reach anyone with the gospel. But the author of Romans 9 sees things from a different angle. Since God is able to have mercy on whomever He will, it is to Him that we should appeal. The Golden Chain of Redemption begins long before any of us are born, but God exists outside of time. We should therefore ask God for His will to include salvation for the people we love. Here in Romans 10, Paul is dealing with Israel in the present tense, in contrast to the chapter 9 discussion of God's election of only some Israelites, which took place in the past.

Despite what he knows about God's election in the past, Paul presently feels compassion for the Jewish people, even those who stridently oppose the gospel message. He, no doubt, remembers the days when he also used to persecute the church with great zeal. Paul remembers that he sincerely believed that he was serving God in so doing. Zeal is an indication of sincerity of belief. Muslims who blow themselves up in service to Allah are obviously sincere in their belief system. The trouble with zeal is not the thing itself. No one criticizes the best three-point shooters in the NBA for being so zealous for their craft that they practice to the point of being extremely good at shooting. They are extremists for a morally neutral cause. All the more, extremists for God ought to be honored, and Paul cites the zeal of the Jews as a reason for his compassionate prayers for them. But zeal without knowledge is not to be honored.

Zeal that is not based on knowledge is a terrible danger. Souls end up in hell, and innocent people die on account of zeal for God that is "not in accordance with knowledge." Knowledge of God comes from two places. First, there is a general revelation given to all humankind. By observing the things that have been made, all people know (although many suppress their knowledge) that there is a God. Nature reveals that there is a God and that He must be very powerful.

Second, God has spoken through the writings of the prophets and apostles. Apostles who oversaw the writing of God's Word (see discussion of Romans 1:1) and prophets who also wrote under the inspiration of the Holy Spirit (Romans 1:2) gave us sixty-six books of special revelation. These special writings must be heeded in order to *know* God. The consistent testimony of all the authors of Scripture is that Jesus is the Christ, the righteous Son of God, and He imputes His righteousness to those who believe in Him. To agree with the prophets and apostles is knowledge.

Every religion besides genuine Christianity is the effort of man to establish his own righteousness. Religious people are zealous to varying degrees as they remain variously faithful to whatever the system. But the systems themselves are manmade creations. The five pillars, the eight-fold path, or even the Ten Commandments are rules to be obeyed in an attempt to establish one's own righteousness. Without knowledge of how God imputes His own righteousness to the person who believes in Jesus, the person who seeks to establish his own righteousness is zealous for the laws of his own system. But "Christ is the end of the law for righteousness to everyone who believes" (Romans 10:4).

31

Salvation

"that if you confess with your mouth Jesus as Lord, and believe in your heart that God raised Him from the dead, you will be saved"

—*Romans 10:9*

Paul is giving the Roman believers a glimpse behind the scenes of heaven in order to provide them with knowledge of God's past, present, and future dealings with Israel. Such knowledge will be the answer to the question of why so many Jewish people do not believe in their own Messiah. But Paul knows that unbelieving Jews will also read his letter. So Paul makes a direct gospel appeal to Jews here in the center of this section (Romans 9-11) that deals with Israel. Paul has told of his prayers for the salvation of the people of Israel. Now God turns Paul into an instrument for answering those prayers. Paul preached *justification through faith* to Jew and Gentile alike (Romans 3:21-5:21), but this outburst of gospel persuasion (Romans 10:5-13) is couched in distinctly Jewish terms. Paul quotes directly from three Old Testament prophets in the space of only nine verses (Moses in Deuteronomy 30:12-14, Isaiah 28:16, and Joel 2:32).

10:5-13   For Moses writes that the man who practices the
                 righteousness which is based on law shall live by that
                 righteousness. But the righteousness based on faith
                 speaks as follows: "DO NOT SAY IN YOUR
                 HEART, 'WHO WILL ASCEND INTO HEAVEN?'
                 (that is, to bring Christ down), or 'WHO WILL
                 DECEND INTO THE ABYSS?' (that is, to bring
                 Christ up from the dead)." But what does it say? "THE
                 WORD IS NEAR YOU, IN YOUR MOUTH AND IN
                 YOUR HEART"—that is, the word of faith which we
                 are preaching, that if you confess with your mouth
                 Jesus as Lord, and believe in your heart that God
                 raised Him from the dead, you will be saved; for with
                 the heart a person believes, resulting in righteousness,
                 and with the mouth he confesses, resulting in
                 salvation. For the Scripture says, "WHOEVER
                 BELIEVES   IN   HIM   WILL   NOT   BE
                 DISAPPOINTED." For there is no distinction between
                 Jew and Greek; for the same Lord is Lord of all,
                 abounding in riches for all who call on Him; for
                 "WHOEVER WILL CALL ON THE NAME OF THE
                 LORD WILL BE SAVED"

These verses are the personification of *justification by faith* as though speaking directly to an unbelieving Jew. As if the gospel itself had a voice, it now calls out to all, but to the Jew especially, because the Jew trusts in his or her obedience to the Law of Moses as a means to being counted righteous. The gospel is appealing to Israelites not to do that. It tells the Jewish person not to think of himself or herself as better than anyone else. *Justification by faith* will present a three-fold persuasion. It rebukes the unbeliever's bad idea, shows how near the good gift is, and extends a simple offer to whoever wants it.

First, the bad idea needs to be debunked. So this gospel presentation begins by explaining that in order to be justified by the Law of Moses, a person would have to obey it perfectly. The inability of individuals to accomplish this is then highlighted in contrast to a better way. The better way is to have faith in Jesus Christ, who is able to accomplish that which sinners cannot do. Can a sinner go up to heaven and bring the Christ down to earth? He cannot, but the baby from Bethlehem was actually the heaven-sent Son of God. Can a sinner go into the grave and raise the Christ? He cannot, but Jesus conquered death itself by rising from the dead. The unbeliever needs to think long and hard about how capable he really is. He cannot do what Jesus has done, so he ought not to think too highly of whatever obedience to the Law of Moses he feels he has accomplished.

Second, whereas perfect obedience to the Law would require the absolute power of God, something that Jesus demonstrated (but you did not), there is something to which you can attain. It is something that is as attainable as speaking a few syllables. The good gift of God is right there under your nose. It is as close as the words that you form with your mouth, provided those words genuinely come from your heart. The rote recitation of a mantra will not save you, but God will give you the gift of His righteousness if you say "Jesus is Lord" and mean it from your heart.

Third, the simple offer is extended without "distinction between Jew and Greek." It is simple because it does not differentiate between people, nor does it complicate the meaning of *faith. Justification by faith* means that righteousness is imputed as a gift to a person only on account of his or her believing in Jesus. *Believing* requires no demonstration, no proof, no work. If a person can only say "Jesus is Lord," understanding who He is and what He has done, simply trusting in Him for salvation, then that person is saved. The idea is nearness. In contrast to the Law that requires so much, the heart can trust in Jesus in an instant. Salvation is only a breath away. One need not ascend to heaven or descend to hell to earn it. One only need confess Jesus as Lord. The offer is left on the table for anyone to call on Jesus.

10:14-15   How then will they call on Him in whom they have not believed? How will they believe in Him whom they have not heard? And how will they hear without a preacher? How will they preach unless they are sent? Just as it is written, "HOW BEAUTIFUL ARE THE FEET OF THOSE WHO BRING GOOD NEWS OF GOOD THINGS!"

Paul the preacher recognizes that what the Holy Spirit just did in him, prompting him to proclaim the gospel (10:5-13), is the hope of Israel. Paul began this section with tears of compassion for a people who are by and large separated from the love of God (9:1-4). He gave us a glimpse of God's sovereign hand working behind the scenes to bring salvation or judgment to whomever He pleases (9:5-29). He revealed that many Gentiles will come to faith, even while few Jews will (9:30-33). Paul will nevertheless be compassionate and pray for every Jew (10:1-4). But unless someone *preaches*, no one will be saved.

In Romans 10:14-15, Paul takes his preaching of the gospel (10:5-13) and multiplies himself a million times over. Every believer in Jesus desires to please our Master. So Paul now touches that desire. He tells us what the Lord Jesus loves to see. It is another glimpse behind the scenes into heaven. Jesus, our Savior and Lord, delights in those who go forth preaching the gospel. The one who carries the good news of salvation has beautiful feet.

But the cooperation of all the members of the body of Christ in the task of preaching the gospel is the actual call of this passage. It is not so much an individual call to preaching as it is a charge to the entire church to value the task and take up the mission. Each one of us should be happy to do our part.

There are two roles that work together to achieve this end. Some are supportive of an intentional effort to reach a group of people. They pray for the effort, encourage people involved in it, and maybe even give items or finances to help the effort. They are *senders*. The sent one ("apostle" actually means "sent one") first of all, has to get to people who do not yet believe in Jesus. Then he has to preach the message of Jesus to the people. The world needs to hear from *preachers*. If the church sends preachers and preachers preach, the people of this world will hear, and some will believe in their hearts and call with their mouths. Salvation is only a breath away, but someone can only speak the word of faith after hearing someone preach, "Jesus is Lord."

32

Broadcast

"So faith comes from hearing, and hearing by the word of Christ"

—Romans 10:17

In the present, the preaching of the gospel is the hope of Israel and the world. Our present task is to preach the good news. The unbelievers' present responsibility is to believe the message of Christ and Him crucified. But the present reality is that most people, and most Israelites in particular, are rejecting God's gospel.

The very fact that the gospel is being preached so far and wide is itself a fulfillment of prophecy and thus a reason why everyone—and Jews in particular—should believe the gospel. Jesus said, "This gospel of the kingdom shall be preached in the whole world as a testimony to all the nations, and then the end will come" (Matthew 24:14). Here in Romans 10:16-21, Paul once again quotes the Old Testament to establish his point because he desires for his Jewish audience to accept its truth. The entire section is essentially a string of quotes. But all of them foretell the worldwide proclamation of the gospel.

10:16-21   However, they did not all heed the good news; for Isaiah says, "LORD, WHO HAS BELIEVED OUR REPORT?" So faith comes from hearing, and hearing

by the word of Christ. But I say, surely they have
never heard, have they? Indeed they have; "THEIR
VOICE HAS GONE OUT INTO ALL THE EARTH,
AND THEIR WORDS TO THE ENDS OF THE
WORLD." But I say, surely Israel did not know did
they? First Moses says, "I WILL MAKE YOU
JEALOUS BY THAT WHICH IS NOT A NATION,
BY A NATION WITHOUT UNDERSTANDING
WILL I ANGER YOU." And Isaiah is very bold and
says, "I WAS FOUND BY THOSE WHO DID NOT
SEEK ME, I BECAME MANIFEST TO THOSE
WHO DID NOT ASK FOR ME." But as for Israel He
says, "ALL THE DAY LONG I HAVE STRETCHED
OUT MY HANDS TO A DISOBEDIENT AND
OBSTINATE PEOPLE."

Paul poses a question from Isaiah 53:1, which just so happens to
be the first verse of perhaps the clearest chapter of Old Testament
prophecy of the Christ. Recall from the discussion of Romans 1:2 that Paul
based the gospel upon the Old Testament prophets. Isaiah 53 speaks about
Jesus Christ in every verse of the chapter, even though it was written more
than seven hundred years before Jesus was incarnated. But Paul quotes the
question from Isaiah 53:1 because this question is what the world and Jews
in particular are faced with. Do you believe that Jesus is the Christ, the Son
of the Living God, who died for our sins and rose from the dead? That is
the question.

The point of reiterating that "faith comes by hearing" the Word of
Christ is that the world is, in fact, hearing us preach, and the only question
that remains is who will believe our report. This was true at the time Paul
wrote Romans, not in the sense that every last soul on the planet had yet
heard the gospel, but in the sense that preachers were going far and wide to
every major city and truly reaching the entire known world. How much
more true is it today? Today, with one hundred million believers in China,
with remote places like Irian Jaya having been reached, with jungle
tribesman like the Auca Indians of Ecuador having embraced Jesus Christ,
who can say that they haven't heard about Jesus Christ? Even though there
are some, the point is that *you* cannot claim ignorance.

Paul's point is particularly geared to the people of Israel. He is
telling them to look at how many Gentiles are accepting the good news.
The faith of the Roman believers was "being proclaimed throughout the
whole world" (Romans 1:8).

That was only possible because God sent the gospel out into the world at precisely the right moment in history, the "fullness of times" (Ephesians 1:10). The Roman Empire specialized in roads, all of which led to Rome, so transportation was possible. The Greek language had pervaded the empire, so communication was possible. And the Pax Romana had provided the peace necessary to travel, especially for a Roman citizen like Paul.

Because God launched the gospel when He did, by His providence, the gospel quickly spread to the entire known world. Meanwhile, most Jewish people were rejecting that gospel. The point is that no one, especially not the Israelites, can claim that lack of opportunity to hear the gospel is an excuse for not believing. On the contrary, that so few Jews were believing was only an indication that in the present time, most of them were "disobedient and obstinate," because the gospel was being held out to them "all the day long."

33

Chosen

*"In the same way then, there has also come to be at the
present time a remnant according to God's gracious
choice"*

—*Romans 11:5*

After Paul's description of the gospel being widely broadcast to the
Jewish people, but mostly rejected by them, someone may wrongly
conclude that God has rejected the Jewish people. So, Paul follows up with
a tremendous summary of the spiritual state of Israel "at the present time,"
meaning as it was when Paul wrote his letter to the Romans. And a strong
case could be made from an observation of history that not much has
changed for almost two thousand years. A monumental physical change
took place for the Jewish people on May 14, 1948, which we will discuss
shortly, but spiritually, Israel has remained in the same condition. Israel is
still a chosen nation, but most Jewish people are in a state of opposition
toward the God who chose them. Meanwhile, God has chosen to soften the
hearts of a small portion of Israel, which individuals He also saves.

11:1-6   I say then, God has not rejected His people, has He?
          May it never be! For I too am an Israelite, a
          descendant of Abraham, of the tribe of Benjamin. God

has not rejected His people whom He foreknew. Or do you not know what the Scripture says in the passage about Elijah, how he pleads with God against Israel? "Lord, THEY HAVE KILLED YOUR PROPHETS, THEY HAVE TORN DOWN YOUR ALTARS, AND I ALONE AM LEFT, AND THEY ARE SEEKING MY LIFE." But what is the divine response to him? "I HAVE KEPT for Myself SEVEN THOUSAND WHO HAVE NOT BOWED THE KNEE TO BAAL." In the same way then, there has also come to be at the present time a remnant according to God's gracious choice. But if it is by grace, it is no longer on the basis of works, otherwise grace is no longer grace.

The promise that God made to Abraham (Genesis 12:1-3) that Israel would be His people remains intact. God has never ceased being faithful to His covenant with Abraham. The Law of Moses, which came 430 years later, has been fulfilled in Christ and now serves a different function than it did before Jesus died and rose from the dead. Supremely, "through the Law comes the knowledge of sin" (Romans 3:20), like a tutor to lead us to Christ, in order that we would be justified by faith in Him (Romans 3:21-25). But God has not set aside His covenant with Israel. May it never be (μή, mé, the stongest Greek negation)! This was an unconditional covenant, and God has remained constant, steadfast in His love for Israel.

Israel, on the other hand, is "at the present time" in the same state of apostasy that it was in during the days of Elijah. Since the time that Moses brought them out of Egypt, only to wander in the desert for forty years, this has essentially been Israel's default position.

Nevertheless, despite the widespread rejection of Yahweh that has always characterized Israel, there have also always been a faithful few who have clung to God, no matter the opposition of their countrymen. According to Jesus, "because narrow is the gate and difficult is the way which leads to life, and there are few who find it" (Matthew 7:14), the current of the river of this world runs decidedly away from God, so those who desire to follow God must do so as the minority. So it has always been with Israel.

Yet, in the days of Elijah, there were seven thousand who refused to bow the knee to Baal. Elijah felt alone, but he was not. The number of true believers—"children of promise" (Romans 9:8)—was small, but not insignificant. So too at the time of Paul, there was an important remnant within Israel that would not bow the knee and proclaim "Caesar is Lord," as Rome later commanded everyone to do, but happily confessed "Jesus is Lord" (Romans 10:9-10), as the obedience of faith compelled Christians to do (Romans 1:5).

So, in summary, God has been faithfully keeping His covenant with Abraham ever since He initiated it. Israel has been an unfaithful covenant partner, but God unconditionally loves them nevertheless. He extends the offer of grace by sending preachers to deliver the gospel to Jews. Most reject because of their stubbornness of heart, but God has mercifully elected a remnant, and He opens their hearts to believe, and so be saved.

11:7-8   What then? What Israel is seeking, it has not obtained, but those who were chosen obtained it, and the rest were hardened; just as it is written, "GOD GAVE THEM A SPIRIT OF STUPOR, EYES TO SEE NOT AND EARS TO HEAR NOT, DOWN TO THIS VERY DAY."

Faith comes at first sight of Jesus Christ. The glory of God that is in His face is utterly compelling. Paul teaches us elsewhere that the devil "has blinded the minds of the unbelieving so that they may not see the light of the gospel of the glory of Christ, who is the image of God" (2 Corinthians 4:4). But here we learn that God *gives them over* to this blindness. In other words, God *allows* Satan to pull this veil over their eyes, so that they are unable to see the glory of Jesus Christ.

How could it be that apart from the remnant "the rest were hardened" (11:7)? Why would God send forth preachers to the farthest reaches of the world and at the same time give a majority of Israelites "a spirit of stupor"? If God makes someone's spiritual eyes blind and their ears deaf, then why send a preacher to tell them at all? More poignantly, is it really fair that He would judge such a spiritually blind person for not believing?

When Paul first addresses this apparent injustice in God in Romans 9:14-18, he makes the point that the softening of a heart is an absolute act of mercy. God will have mercy on whom He chooses to have mercy (9:15), but He does not owe it to anyone. All of humanity has together become unrighteous, and were God to judge the whole lot of us (or any one of us), He would be perfectly righteous in so doing. Mercy cannot be demanded.

But the hardening of a heart is an opposite activity of God. It is one thing to say that God mercifully softens a heart. It is another to say that He actively makes a heart hard. In order to understand the parallel language, it is essential to consider the example that Paul gives to explain the point. Pharaoh is the one that Paul cites to demonstrate that God "hardens whom He desires" (9:18). In the account of God's story found in Exodus, God is presented as the active Deliverer of Israel. It is only secondarily a story about Moses, an instrument in God's hand, or Pharaoh, an opponent to God's hand.

The point of the story is not simply that God will overcome the powers of evil. Of course, that is the case. God is omnipotent. Who could have stopped Him from getting His people out of Israel? But God had an even bigger sovereign plan. Not only would God save Israel, He would do it the way He desired. That included plagues against Egypt, each one demonstrating His power over the false gods of Egypt. They worshipped Pharaoh as a sun god. God sent Moses as a type of the Son of God—Jesus Christ.

The various plagues demonstrated Yahweh's superiority over the imagined gods of Egypt. He turned the Nile River to blood, sent frogs throughout the land, and in every practical way proved that the gods of Egypt were not gods at all. But most importantly, Pharaoh had to resist right up until the last plague—the death of the firstborn. Otherwise, the most crucial event would not have happened. The blood of lambs was placed on the doorposts of the Israelites. This blood pre-figured the blood of Jesus—the Lamb of God. When an angel of death passed through Egypt, he passed over Israel and did not execute judgment against her sin. For fifteen hundred years until the true Passover Lamb came, Israel remembered this event through the Passover Festival. And all of this was part of God's sovereign plan to bring the Christ into the world. What fool would resist the power of God right up until the tenth plague? Pharaoh's heart was just that hard because God was executing His sovereign plan.

So how is that fair to Pharaoh, to be used like a pawn in God's cosmic scheme? To answer that question, we must first understand the nature of the process of *hardening*. The text of Exodus underscores Paul's point in Romans 9:14-18 that those whom God hardens are in no way righteous. Before Exodus tells us that God hardened Pharaoh's heart, which it does many times, we are first told that Pharaoh hardened his heart against God.

If God at any point chooses to stop extending grace to any individual, then the heart of that person will continue unabated on the course it was already on. God does not need to actively make someone oppose Him. Rather, those who oppose God, especially His rescue plan for humanity, are actively hardening their own hearts against God. If God stops restraining their evil, He hardens them further in a sense, but not in an active sense. The author of evil in the human heart is human, and the spirit who inspires this hardness is the devil (2 Corinthians 4:4). God is not the author of sin, but for the establishment of His sovereign purposes, He may give people over to their own sin. Recall the three-fold "gave them over" repetition of Romans 1. When people exchange the glory of God for a lie and make idols for themselves, God is free to give them over to the desires of their own hearts. He does that for His own purposes.

11:9-10   And David says, "LET THEIR TABLE BECOME A SNARE AND A TRAP, AND A STUMBLING BLOCK AND A RETRIBUTION TO THEM. LET THEIR EYES BE DARKENED TO SEE NOT, AND BEND THEIR BACKS FOREVER."

Faith in Jesus Christ is not blind. It is a kind of seeing. To behold the glory of the Son of God is not a vain human imagination, but a vision of a reality as Jesus Christ actually is. What's more, it does not require a blind leap to arrive at this vision. Rather, everything necessary to accept this reality was prophesied hundreds of years before He came. To believe in Jesus is to accept the only logical explanation for the revelation of God. In a general sense, one need only observe nature, especially the human being, and know that there is a God. So the idea that God could take on flesh, perform miracles, and even rise from the dead does not require an illogical imagination. Rather, it fits perfectly within the construct of a created world that can only come from an all-powerful Creator.

In a specific sense, that the world was created through Jesus Christ, who was with God in the beginning and is Himself God (John 1:1) should be easily acceptable because sixty-six books testify uniformly to this reality, as if forty different authors separated by fifteen hundred years were the Voice of One. The things that the prophets foretold and the apostles recounted cannot be explained away. The only explanation for the Bible is that Jesus is the Son of God.

Paul is not vindictive toward those who reject Jesus Christ. His tears (9:1-5) and prayers (10:1) eliminate the possibility of that being the case. Rather, he quotes David here in Romans 11:9-10 because what David says is true.

Anyone who rejects the revelation of God, turning their eyes away from the One whom the preacher glorifies, is in grave danger of being granted his or her own choice. The Jewish person in particular in this passage is pretending that Jesus is not the Christ. They are setting this table for themselves. Their table will "become a snare and a trap, and a stumbling block and a retribution to them" the instant that God withdraws His Spirit of grace and allows them to believe their own lies. They cover their eyes with their arms and plug their ears with their fingers. God may allow their eyes to go totally blind and their ears to go deaf, and if so, then the weight of their sin will "bend their backs forever."

34

Future

"Now if their transgression is riches for the world and their failure is riches for the Gentiles, how much more will their fulfillment be!"

Romans 11:12

Romans 9 revealed God's dealings with Israel in the past (election before any individual Jew had done either well or badly). Romans 10:1-11:10 revealed God's dealing with Israel in the present (holding out the gospel to them all the day long, but a majority hardened in their hearts to it). Now Romans 11:11-36 reveals how God will deal with Israel in the future.

11:11-16   I say then, they did not stumble so as to fall, did they? May it never be! But by their transgression salvation has come to the Gentiles, to make them jealous. Now if their transgression is riches for the world and their failure is riches for the Gentiles, how much more will their fulfillment be! But I am speaking to you who are Gentiles. Inasmuch then as I am an apostle of Gentiles, I magnify my ministry, if somehow I might move to jealousy my fellow countrymen and save some of

them. For if their rejection is the reconciliation of the
world, what will their acceptance be but life from the
dead? If the first piece of dough is holy, the lump is
also; and if the root is holy, the branches are too.

The question is whether the by and large rejection of the Christ by
the nation of Israel is the kind of fall from which Israel will never get back
up. Israel had a long history of falling into apostasy. In the book of Judges,
they fell into apostasy as many times as God sent a deliverer to reclaim
them. They cycled between falling away from God and returning to Him.
But is this time different? Have they rejected their ultimate Deliverer and
no other shall be sent?

They have rejected their Savior. No other will be sent. But
amazingly (grace is always amazing), God still has a plan to extend mercy
to Israel, to soften their hearts, and to bring His nation (by and large) back
to Himself one more time! Was the fall final and fatal? Paul answers with
the strongest Greek negation (μή, mé). May it never be!

This time with regard to the future, God gives us another
astonishing glimpse behind the scenes of heaven. There we see the
sovereign hand of God working to bring about amazing purposes in the
lives of individuals and in the course of the nations. He is working all
things together for His glory and for the joy of those who love Him
(Romans 8:28).

There is now a time of the Gentiles whereby billions of non-Jews
will come to faith in Christ and be included in God's eternal family. The
children of God by descent from Abraham are children of promise only if
they believe in Jesus. These are the remnant who are part of the church all
along. But the nation of Israel is being provoked as long as greater and
greater numbers of people across this world turn to accept their Messiah—
the same One whom the Jewish people reject. They see our lives. They see
the fruit of the Holy Spirit in our lives. They rub up against us and are
jealous of the joy of the Lord that they see in us, which satisfaction in God
they know that they do not have.

It was always God's plan to bless the whole world through the
Jewish Messiah (Genesis 12:3). But the Messiah was first of all Jewish. He
was offered first to them. Had they truly welcomed Him instead of
crucifying Him a week after He made His triumphal entry into
Jerusalem—the capital of His kingdom, He would have ruled over them
and judged the world from the place of His throne (Isaiah 11:1-4). But of
course such hypothetical scenarios are only academic, since God always
planned, even before the creation of the world, that the Lamb would be

slain (Revelation 13:8). The big idea of Romans 9-11 is that God is sovereign over all that happens and no less over the present time rejection of their Messiah by the Jewish people. Nevertheless, Jesus was genuinely presented to Israel as her king (Matthew 21:1-11) and her rejection of Him meant that He would die for Jew and Gentile alike. God now *wants* Jews to be jealous of the many Gentiles who now accept their Messiah.

Most Jews now harden themselves against that jealousy, ignoring the fact that the message of the Jewish Messiah is running to the farthest reaches of this planet. Every Australian, Russian, Brazilian, and Canadian who comes to Jesus brings God glory. There are millions of each coming. Glory upon glory to God. But how abundant our joy will be, and how we will praise Him and give Him glory when the blessing that came to the world through Abraham turns back around and blesses Abraham's descendants. In every generation, individual Jews are free to be completed by their Messiah. But when the nation of Israel turns (by and large) to their Messiah, it will be like life from the dead. How fitting that the Representative Israel—Jesus Christ, the perfect son of Abraham, the perfect son of David—died and rose from the dead, and there is coming a day when the nation of Israel, which is currently dead to God (John 3:36), will rise from the dead and live.

Individual Jews who presently believe in Jesus Christ are completed Jews. But there are few of them compared to the majority who disbelieve. The Messianic Jews during these times of the Gentiles are "the first piece of dough." The whole lump will eventually follow. There is already a holy root that is Israel. These Jewish believers preach the gospel day and night. They are the Elijahs and Pauls of our day. The remnant is enough to keep the root alive. The branches will be added soon.

35

Branches

*"And they also, if they do not continue in their unbelief, will
be grafted in, for God is able to graft them in again"*

—*Romans 11:23*

The analogy of the olive tree involves true Israel as the root,
unbelieving Jews as broken-off branches, and believing Gentiles as
grafted-in branches. Agriculturalists will understand the analogy more
easily, but the crucial point to understand is that good branches bear fruit,
but they depend on a good root for their life. Typically, if a branch does
not bear fruit, the gardener will cut it off. An olive-producing branch can
be cut and tied into place on the spot where the bad branch was removed.
A gardener can graft branches to maximize production of olives. But it is
unusual for him to go find branches from a wild olive tree somewhere.
One would think that the gardener would keep to his garden, but God's
garden turns out to be bigger than Israel.

11:17-24　　But if some of the branches were broken off, and you,
being a wild olive, were grafted in among them and
became partaker with them of the rich root of the olive
tree, do not be arrogant toward the branches; but if you
are arrogant, remember that it is not you who supports

the root, but the root supports you. You will say then, "Branches were broken off so that I might be grafted in." Quite right, they were broken off for their unbelief, but you stand by your faith. Do not be conceited, but fear; for if God did not spare the natural branches, He will not spare you either. Behold then the kindness and severity of God; to those who fell, severity, but to you, God's kindness, if you continue in His kindness; otherwise you also will be cut off. And they also, if they do not continue in their unbelief, will be grafted in, for God is able to graft them in again. For if you were cut off from what is by nature a wild olive tree, and were grafted contrary to nature into a cultivated olive tree, how much more will these who are the natural branches be grafted into their own olive tree?

One should not press the analogy too far. There is not a one-to-one correspondence between the branches that get cut off and the places available for branches to be grafted in. Every Israelite who is cut off from Christ is removed from the tree. But regardless of how many are removed, the root is big enough and strong enough to support however many Gentiles that God would desire to graft in.

So what remained of the root when the Old Testament gave way to the New Testament? Paul opened this past, present, future discourse concerning Israel (Romans 9-11) with a lament for those who are cut off when it doesn't have to be that way. In Romans 9:1-5, Paul grieves the fact that so many Jews are rejecting Jesus. What made Israel special was not destroyed. The root is still there. The root includes "the adoption as sons, and the glory and the covenants and the giving of the law and the temple service and the promises" (9:4). The root remembers the fathers and focuses especially on the "Christ according to the flesh, who is over all, God blessed forever" (9:5). Israel, including all of these special blessings, is the root that lives on. The remnant still lives among us, and they are living branches. But the whole nation, as many as the stars in the sky (Genesis 12:1-3), centralized again in Israel although still spread out like a canopy across the nations of the earth, should be honored as the root into which believing Gentiles have been grafted.

Gentile believers had better remember that the root supports them. They are not the root, but only branches that God in His amazing mercy chose to graft in. If any Gentile professes to believe in the Christ and yet despises, persecutes, or opposes the nation of Israel, then he or she needs to tremble before God. God's severity is reserved for such a person. How can he or she claim to love God and yet hate God's chosen people (1 John 4:20)? Some Israelites may be cut-off branches and therefore not brothers in Christ, but with regard to the promise of God, they are still children of the flesh of Abraham. The whole nation of Israel is important in the grand plan of God as He works out that plan in history. So, the one who cuts at the root may look back and find that he or she was never truly grafted into Christ in the first place. Anti-Semitism should not be found in a Christian. If a person finds it in his heart, then he should question his own salvation.

But let us not lose sight of the marvelous point of the olive tree analogy. God is able to bring Gentiles to believe in the Jewish Messiah, so it will an easy thing for Him to soften the hearts of the nation of Israel and graft them back into their own tree. There is coming a day when the nation of Israel will be a believing nation. History has shown that God has brought billions of Gentiles into the tree. The tree is ready and able to support an influx of Jewish believers. It is a natural thing for this revival to happen. Do not be surprised when the nation of Israel begins to turn en masse to the Jewish Messiah.

36

Irrevocable

"for the gifts and the calling of God are irrevocable"

—Romans 11:29

A biblical mystery is something that was previously undisclosed that God is now making known. Gentile believers must not look down upon Jewish unbelievers because the mystery now revealed is that "all Israel will be saved." What we can presently observe with our eyes, namely that most Jews reject the Messiah, will not be the reality forever. The future holds a massive softening of Israelite hearts. They will be shown mercy in the Romans 9:14-18 sense of the term. Their hearts will be softened in the future, and to a magnitude at least as great as their hearts are hard at the present time. In the dark ages of anti-Semitic European history, Catholic theologians and even Protestants like Martin Luther did not appreciate this teaching in its fullness. Many tried to apply the gifts and calling of Israel, which irrevocably belong to Israel, to the church. Israel was thus ignored or even denigrated. This was a grievous error on the part of those theologians, but not altogether impossible to understand since Israel no longer existed as a nation.

But today we must not fall into the same error. On May 14, 1948 Israel was reborn as a nation. It was no coincidence that the events that led to the rebirth of the nation included the worst episode of anti-Semitism the world has ever witnessed. Strongly influenced by the liberal teachings of Friedrich Schleiermacher, Albert Schweitzer and other German higher critics, especially Adolf Von Harnack, Germany by and large departed from belief in the Bible. A remnant called the Confessing Church led by ministers like Dietrich Bonhoeffer opposed the rise of the Nazis. But Hitler did seize power, and the Holocaust was soon written into history.

It was not the first time in history that world powers attempted the complete destruction of the Jewish people. No other people have been targeted for genocide like the Jews. From the Pharaoh of ancient Egypt to the Persian potentate during the time of Esther to the radical Muslim cleric of today, Israel has always had a target on its back.

But why? Israel is the apple of God's eye (Zechariah 2:8) and the key instrument through which God brings about His purposes on earth (Daniel 9-12), so the spirit that is at work in the sons of disobedience (Ephesians 2:2) will inspire zeal without knowledge in opposition to Israel.

Despite being the world's target for persecution, the nation of Israel rose from the death of the Holocaust to restore the children of Abraham's flesh to the Land of Promise. That the nation of Israel was literally born into the land of Israel on a specific day was a fulfillment of prophecy. Like the sixty-six books of the Bible, Isaiah has sixty-six chapters. Significant to the point that Israel is reborn as a nation at the end of time, in Isaiah's last chapter, he prophesied the event that took place on May 14, 1948. The sixty-sixth book of the Bible is largely the story of God's end-time dealings with the nation of Israel. In the Book of Revelation (7:4-8), God anoints 144,000 Jews, 12,000 from each of the 12 tribes, to receive a seal of His protection and go forth preaching repentance and faith to the ends of the earth just prior to the triumphal return of King Jesus.

Israel is the woman who gave the Christ to world (Revelation 12:1-5). According to Isaiah, "Before she travailed, she brought forth; before her pain came, she gave birth to a boy" (Isaiah 66:7). Jesus came into the world during the Pax Romana—the peace of Rome. Israel was prospering under the wicked King Herod, Jerusalem flourishing architecturally, financially, and by every worldly standard. As the Baby was laid in Bethlehem's manger, the bustling city only took notice of Herod's displeasure and the disruption of their worldly peace (Matthew 2:3). No one but a few shepherds and later some Gentile Magi took proper notice of the true King of Peace brought forth just five miles outside the City of Peace.

Little did Israel know the travail and pain that was about to come upon her. In normal childbirth, the pain precedes the delivery. But the birth of the Deliverer came before Israel's travail and pain, as a sign to the nations looking back now upon the words of the prophet. Isaiah spoke correctly because Israel's travail began not long after Jesus was born in 70 AD when the Roman Empire ransacked the City of Peace. Israel was driven into diaspora and would not regather as a nation until May 14, 1948. This brings us to the next verse of Isaiah's prophecy.

"Who has heard such a thing? Who has seen such things? Can a land be born in one day? Can a nation be brought forth all at once? As soon as Zion travailed, she also brought forth her sons" (Isaiah 66:8). The birthing travail of Israel reached its climax in the Holocaust and subsequent suffering that found no relief until that miracle of days, May 14, 1948, when a land was born in a day and a nation was brought forth all at once. It was the first true deliverance of Israel since 70 AD.

Consider how utterly unique and amazing this occurrence was. There has never been a dispersed nation that retained its identity for more than four or five generations after being scattered from their land. Think of how amazing it is. Is there any chance in your mind that the Native Americans who were sent away down the Trail of Tears are about to return back up the Trail to retake possession of any land they lost? It is impossible, since that particular Native American tribe has been largely absorbed into the United States, and the reservations that exist are dedicated land. A return east for this tribe's descendants to places where homes and businesses are held as private property is unthinkable.

How much greater a miracle is the return in 1948 of a people who were dispersed in 70 AD. Having accomplished this miracle, is there any doubt that God will see the rebirth of Israel through to completion, whereby the nation of Israel comes to be known as completed Jews? Will the reborn nation not soon find their own Messiah?

As Isaiah put the question, "'Shall I bring to the point of birth and not give delivery?' says the Lord. 'Or shall I who gives delivery shut the womb?' says your God" (Isaiah 66:9). Israel was born as a nation into the land. Is there not a coming revival whereby a majority of Jews in the land are going to be "born again" (John 3:3)? The new birth is spiritual. Without it, individuals will never enter the Kingdom of God. But God's program with Israel, according to the irrevocable covenant of God, also includes the promise of a land (Genesis 12:1). Israel as a nation has now been reborn into the land of promise. A vast number of spiritual rebirths is coming to Israel in the not-too-distant future.

11:25-32   For I do not want you, brethren, to be uninformed of this mystery—so that you will not be wise in your own estimation—that a partial hardening has happened to Israel until the fullness of the Gentiles has come in, and so all Israel will be saved; just as it is written, "THE DELIVERER WILL COME FROM ZION, HE WILL REMOVE UNGODLINESS FROM JACOB. THIS IS MY COVENANT WITH THEM, WHEN I TAKE AWAY THEIR SINS." From the standpoint of the gospel they are enemies for your sake, but from the standpoint of God's choice they are beloved for the sake of the fathers; for the gifts and the calling of God are irrevocable. For just as you once were disobedient to God, but now have been shown mercy because of their disobedience, so these also now have been disobedient, that because of the mercy shown to you they also may now be shown mercy. For God has shut up all in disobedience so that He may show mercy to all.

To be "shown mercy" in the context of Romans 9-11 is to have one's heart softened, so as to believe in Jesus and thus be saved. We are told that "all Israel will be saved", that God "will remove ungodliness from Jacob" (Jacob being another name for Israel), and that God will "take away their sins." So, it is clear that God is planning a national spiritual revival for the Jewish people.

Like Isaiah did, Ezekiel foresaw the return of the Jewish people to the land. He described a valley of dry bones (Ezekiel 38), and he marveled when the Lord revealed that these dry bones would once again live. He said that they were the whole house of Israel and the whole house of Judah. Significantly, at the time of Ezekiel the kingdom of Israel was divided between these two houses. But Ezekiel was told to write the name of each on two sticks and symbolically join the two together. He was told that this prophetic symbol indicated that the two houses would once again be united as one nation in the land. That would have seemed impossible in Ezekiel's day. But today ever since May 14, 1948, it is the reality. From north to south, Israel exists as one undivided nation. They await the arrival of the King.

King Jesus obviously knew all this would happen. Similar to Paul's analogy of the root and branches, Jesus told us to learn something about Israel. In the Old Testament, Israel was commonly likened to the fig tree (Hosea 9:10, 10:1, 14:6, Isaiah 5:1-7, Psalm 80:9, Jeremiah 11:16). Jesus said, "Now learn the parable of the fig tree: when its branch has already become tender and puts forth its leaves, you know that summer is near; so, you too, when you see all these things, recognize that He is near, right at the door. Truly I say to you, this generation will not pass away until all these things take place" (Matthew 24:32-34).

The word translated "generation" here (γενεά, genea) often refers to a race or family, not always a generation (a period of forty years or so). Exactly as Jesus said, the Jewish race did not disappear despite almost two thousand years of exile. In our day, we are seeing Israel—the fig tree— "become tender and put forth its leaves." Before 1948, there was little to no life in the land. But the first tender life began in 1948, and even today, Jews are returning en masse to the land. We ought to take Jesus' prophecy seriously and recognize that "He is near, right at the door" and nothing is going to be able to remove Israel from the land, even though surrounding nations threaten to drive her into the sea.

When all these prophecies are taken together, it becomes clear that God was at work in bringing His chosen people back into the Promised Land and He is going to turn their hearts back to Him as well. We are not told when the revival will occur, but since the book of Revelation seems to speak of the same events, it appears that it will occur just prior to the return of Jesus. The promises of God are sure, even though we don't have a complete understanding of how everything will play out.

37

Doxology

"Oh, the depth of the riches both of the wisdom and knowledge of God! How unsearchable are His judgments and unfathomable His ways!"

—Romans 11:33

Paul closes this amazing glimpse behind the scenes of heaven with a beautiful doxology. In chapters 9-11, we have been shown the sovereign hand of God. This glimpse behind the scenes showed us a lot about Israel. But God's dealings with Israel also shed much light upon His dealings with all people. God mercifully elects some to salvation, but chooses to pass over others. He softens hearts and He hardens hearts. He does the latter by withdrawing His merciful hand and allowing the wicked human heart to follow its natural course. The sovereign work that God does upon the human heart does not eliminate a real sense in which people freely choose to either accept or reject Christ. God genuinely holds His hand out to everyone.

Someone has rightly said that the gate that leads into heaven is inscribed with a sign. As the believer approaches, the sign reads, "Whosoever will may enter." But after the believer passes through and looks back over his or her shoulder, the sign reads "Chosen from the foundation of the world." How it is that these two things could both be true is beyond us, but then again, why would we think that our tiny human brains could fully comprehend the infinite mind of God?

11:33-36   Oh, the depths of the riches both of the wisdom and knowledge of God! How unsearchable are His judgments and unfathomable His ways! For WHO HAS KNOWN THE MIND OF THE LORD, OR WHO BECAME HIS COUNSELOR? OR WHO HAS FIRST GIVEN TO HIM THAT IT MIGHT BE PAID BACK TO HIM AGAIN? For from Him and through Him and to Him are all things. To Him be the glory forever. Amen.

In the past, God elected those upon whom He desired to have mercy. Even though the Israelites are the chosen children of God, there exist within the nation both children of promise and children of flesh. Like the clay should refrain from questioning the potter, we are in no position to question why God does not save all people. But we are told that none of us deserve His mercy. Those He saves owe it all to His grace. Those who end up under His judgment are not there because of any lack of love in God. Rather, He genuinely holds out His hand to them all the day long, but they prove themselves disobedient and obstinate. The congruence of human responsibility and divine sovereignty is very difficult to understand. So, we must rest with the knowledge He gives and in the end recognize "how unsearchable are His judgments and unfathomable His ways!"

With regard to the present, we know that Israel is experiencing a hardening in part for a time according to the sovereign purposes of God. Nevertheless, today is the day of salvation for every Jew who is willing to come. The same gospel that is offered to Gentiles is also offered to them. So, we must pray like Paul (10:1) and preach the gospel like him (10:5-13) with real hope that faith will come by hearing. We are the senders and the preachers who take the gospel to Jew and Gentile alike. But pray as we do, we cannot be God's counselor, and we cannot perfectly discern His mind, so we must always trust in the God who saves. We can sleep at night, despite our abiding sorrow for the lost, knowing that He sits on the throne.

With regard to the future, how glorious is the truth that Israel has been reborn into the Land of Promise and is on the verge of a national turning to Messiah. "I will pour out on the house of David and on the inhabitants of Jerusalem, the Spirit of grace and supplication, so that they will look on Me whom they have pierced; and they will mourn for Him, as one mourns for an only son, and they will weep bitterly over Him like the bitter weeping over the firstborn" (Zechariah 12:10). Jesus is the Son whom they pierced. The Wailing Wall, the western wall of the Temple where the Jews pray to this day, is soon to be turned into a place of supplication where the Jewish people come to call on Jesus Christ to return from heaven. Oh, the glory of this mystery now revealed! And still so far beyond our tracing out.

Jesus Christ is the glorious Son of God. A glimpse of heaven is therefore a glimpse of Him. The hand of God in history is the working together of all things to bring glory to the name of Jesus. Truly Jesus is the name above every name (Philippians 2:5-11). Jesus is the source and the continuance and the destination of all things. As Paul says, "from Him and through Him and to Him are all things. To Him be the glory forever. Amen" (Romans 11:36). We saw a glimpse of His sovereignty, and so we end this section in the same posture with which we started, looking up at the Christ, "who is over all, God blessed forever. Amen" (Romans 9:5).

SECTION 6

Good Principles for a Godly Life

Romans 12:1-15:13

38

Worship

"Therefore I urge you, brethren, by the mercies of
God, to present your bodies a living and holy
sacrifice, acceptable to God, which is your
spiritual service of worship"

—*Romans 12:1*

The book of Romans located us in the jungle of sin. It is a jungle so deep that we have no hope of escaping, no hope of making it home. All people are in the same predicament. We are knee deep in mud, dirty with sin, and blind to our condition. We think we can help ourselves. We assume that we'll make a way out, but we are the walking dead.

The book of Romans not only shone a light upon us to open our eyes to our desperate condition. In an instant ("but now" in 3:21), it revealed the glory of Jesus Christ and manifested His righteousness upon the lost sinner. The sinner only needs to believe in Jesus, beholding the manifold beauty of the gospel, in order to be justified. God declares us righteous, right where we stand, on account of our faith in His Son.

The book of Romans then gave us a new vision of the new people we became in that moment when we first believed. Rather than the mirror of God's law, which shows us how sinful we are, the waters of baptism reflect an image of people who are dead to sin and alive in Christ. The old sinful nature will still hang around us and will torment us like a dead dog that inexplicably comes to life from time to time to wage war against the new spiritual man. We must yield ourselves to God's Holy Spirit in us, once again consider our old nature to be dead, and trust the never-failing love of God to keep us safe from sin until that soon-coming day when we will be rescued out of the jungle and our old sin nature will trouble us no more.

The book of Romans never wants us to get too caught up in ourselves, so before giving us practical instructions to follow as we journey in the jungle for a short time, it turns our eyes to heaven to see Whose hand truly governs the world. The ultimate issue in the unfolding of history on earth is the eternal destiny of the people that God placed here in the world.

Since Israel is His special race of people, and since the world notices that most of them are not accepting their Christ, God reveals key aspects of His dealing with them as a particular example of how His plans govern the entire world. In the past, He elected those who would be saved. In the present, the gospel is genuinely offered to Jew and Gentile alike. In the future, a great acceptance of the gospel in the nation of Israel is due to come. By showing us a glimpse of heaven before sending us out to walk in the jungle, we can remember His sovereign control over everything, including the terribly painful things that come our way. We can be assured that He is working all things together for our joy and His glory.

So now, the time to walk has finally arrived. We now know where we are. We know we have been born again. We know that the Holy Spirit must guide our walk. We know that the hand of God allows every circumstance that we will face. So we begin to move as new creations in the same old sin-cursed world.

As we go, what tripping hazards do we need to watch out for? What principles need to direct our decision-making? Where do we go from here? We observe practical principles of Christian living. Since God has declared us "good," we ought to live by good principles.

12:1-2   Therefore I urge you, brethren, by the mercies of God, to present your bodies a living and holy sacrifice, acceptable to God, which is your spiritual service of worship. And do not be conformed to this world, but be transformed by the renewing of your mind, so that you may prove what the will of God is, that which is good and acceptable and perfect.

The overarching principle by which Christians are to live is that we use our bodies to honor God. Everything we do has now become an opportunity to worship. Our minds are to think about how to bring about His will in the world. Our brains are for worship. The carpenter who builds houses must labor as if the house he is building will belong to the Lord. Our hands are for worship. The radio talk show host must speak in such a way as to make the world a home for the Lord. Our lips are for worship. "Whether, then, you eat or drink or whatever you do, do all to the glory of God" (1 Corinthians 10:31).

We ought to devote special days entirely to singing praise, praying, and reading the Bible, but in light of who God is and what He has done for us and in us, our reasonable service of worship is to devote every minute of every day to Him. We should seek to please Him from the most mundane to the most profound moments of our lives.

As we go, we are growing as disciples in the truth. The newborn Christian will not walk as steadily as the mature seasoned veteran believer. But as we seek to live a life of worship, we must recognize that two countervailing forces are working upon us. We are passive with reference to them, meaning that they are actively operating upon us all the time, not the other way around.

First, the world is trying to press us into its mold. The world refers to the culture at large, everything from music to shows to jokes to values. It is not "the man" or governments or any particular institution. It includes all of those things, but is actually empowered and unified in purpose by none other than Satan. He is the "god of this world" (2 Corinthians 4:4) who seeks to blind eyes to the glory of Jesus. Jesus is the One to whom we are seeking to offer our bodies as a spiritual service of worship, but the world will have none of it.

The second force is the power of the Holy Spirit as He works within us to transform our minds to think and be like Christ. We are passive in the sense that He is the One with the power to actually change us. Our own behavior modification will not be particularly effective. Rather as we relate to the Holy Spirit, as we learn to discern His voice, as we submit to Him, He changes us from the inside out. As we walk in the Spirit, we may not be able to tell someone where we are going in life, what activity we will be doing in five years. But day by day, we become aware that we are in the center of God's will. We will see His hand of providence leading us every step of the way.

39

Church

"so we, who are many, are one body in Christ, and individually members one of another"

—*Romans 12:5*

U p until this point in the book of Romans, the text has been largely about God and the individual. It is crucial to understand that sin (1:18-3:20), salvation (3:21-5:21), sanctification (6-8), and election (9-11) concern individuals, not groups. No young woman will go to heaven just because her parents are believers. Conversely, even if a Muslim family in a 99% Muslim country raised a Muslim boy, his relationship with God is a stewardship between the created boy and his Creator and no one else. Each person will either languish in hell or delight in heaven based on whether or not he or she believes in Jesus Christ. But once saved, the Christian needs to understand right away that he or she was saved into the church.

12:3-8   For through the grace given to me I say to everyone among you not to think more highly of himself than he ought to think; but to think so as to have sound judgment, as God has allotted to each a measure of faith. For just as we have many members in one body and all the members do not have the same function, so

> we, who are many, are one body in Christ, and
> individually members one of another. Since we have
> gifts that differ according to the grace given to us,
> each of us is to exercise them accordingly: if
> prophecy, according to the proportion of his faith; if
> service, in his serving; or he who teaches, in his
> teaching; or he who exhorts, in his exhortation; he who
> gives, with liberality; he who leads, with diligence; he
> who shows mercy, with cheerfulness.

Like adding living stones to a spiritual temple (1 Peter 2:4-6), God saves individual people, but only to add them to something much larger than the individual. The church is the body of Christ. Like a human body that has hands, feet, eyes and ears, the church needs all Christians to fulfill the role for which he or she was made.

The first key necessary for the newborn man to operate well in the church is to "not think more highly of himself than he ought to think." The old sinful nature loves to prod a man's pride. The first thing that a new believer should be thinking about is not how to get on TBN or fill a stadium with fans of his powerful preaching. God will raise up spokesmen in His church, but each believer needs to focus on how he or she can truly serve the church in the best way.

The second key is discovering what spiritual gifts the Holy Spirit has deposited within a person to enable him or her to serve the church. No special gifting should be a source of pride for the person who has it. Each one comes from the Holy Spirit, not from the person who has the gift. Spiritual gifts are not earned. God gives them by His grace as He desires.

Once saved, having been justified through faith, the new believer ought to be baptized by the local church in which he intends to serve. The baptism of the Spirit included the believer in the universal church, which is made up of every person who has ever trusted in Jesus Christ unto salvation. Since only God knows the heart, only He knows for sure who those people are. Since the baptism of the Spirit is invisible and the identity of those who "were made to drink of one Spirit" (1 Corinthians 12:13) is not entirely known to us, theologians have used the term "invisible church" to describe the true universal church. But baptism with water is an intentionally visible and public act. It identifies a believer with Jesus Christ, and secondarily, it ought to identify him or her with a local church. Ideally, the believer should continue in the fellowship of the Bible-believing gospel-preaching church that baptized him or her.

After baptism, the believer should then immediately begin serving. The church will make decisions together about who preaches on Sunday mornings, who teaches what classes, and who offers instruction in the things of the Lord. Elders in the church must safeguard the doctrine (Titus 1:9). But for the sake of the body of Christ, each believer should look to contribute in any way he or she can. Whether that means cleaning, setting up chairs, running wires for sound equipment, or trying to meet and encourage people in the church, the new believer ought to be a churchman from day one of his new life in Christ.

40

Love

*"Let love be without hypocrisy. Abhor what
is evil; cling to what is good"*

—Romans 12:9

We are saved through faith, but we are saved to love. Love must be sincere. Our love for God and our love for neighbor will be the first evidence that salvation really happened to us. Hypocrisy originally referred to actors on a stage who would hold masks over their faces that depicted various emotions. The mask did not reveal what was really in the actor's heart, only what the actor wanted the audience to think of the character he was portraying. Unlike hypocritical actors, Christians need to focus on genuinely loving God and people.

12:9-13   Let love be without hypocrisy. Abhor what is evil; cling to what is good. Be devoted to one another in brotherly love; give preference to one another in honor; not lagging behind in diligence, fervent in spirit, serving the Lord; rejoicing in hope, persevering in tribulation, devoted to prayer, contributing to the needs of the saints, practicing hospitality.

If we love God, then we will abhor what is evil and cling to what is good. We must actively train our brains by submitting to the Holy Spirit to hate things like drunkenness, selfish spending habits, cursing, or any kind of sexual sin, like pornography, or any of the twenty-one other examples of sin listed in Romans 1. Since God hates these things, we should also, because we love God. Likewise, we should love the things God loves.

God supremely loves people. He loves people so much that He gave His only Son to take on flesh and become one of us! What's more, the Scripture highlights how one-sided His love is. "But God demonstrates His own love toward us, in that while we were yet sinners, Christ died for us" (Romans 5:8).

Since God so loves people, we should therefore seek to love our neighbors as ourselves. This is especially true of our relationships with people in our churches. We should not allow our friendships to be just something that we can take or leave. We should truly be devoted to others. We should not be lazy, but work hard so that we have something to contribute. We should have fun together. We should cry together when we suffer and seek to bear each other's burdens. We should take time for prayer meetings and remember each other in prayer when we are apart. We should give to the poor. Our homes should frequently be open to entertain guests. Love for God manifests in love for people, and if it is sincere, then it will be expressed in practical ways.

12:14-21	Bless those who persecute you; bless and do not curse. Rejoice with those who rejoice, and weep with those who weep. Be of the same mind toward one another, do not be haughty in mind, but associate with the lowly. Do not be wise in your own estimation. Never pay back evil for evil to anyone. Respect what is right in the sight of all men. If possible, so far as it depends on you, be at peace with all men. Never take your own revenge, beloved, but leave room for the wrath of God, for it is written, "VENGEANCE IS MINE, I WILL REPAY," says the Lord. "BUT IF YOUR ENEMY IS HUNGRY, FEED HIM, AND IF HE IS THIRSTY, GIVE HIM A DRINK; FOR IN SO DOING YOU WILL HEAP BURNING COALS ON HIS HEAD." Do not be overcome by evil, but overcome evil with good.

Particular kinds of people are in need of particular expressions of love. The first example given in this section (12:14-21) is our enemies. How we treat our enemies will most clearly distinguish Christian love from merely human love. Whereas worldly wisdom would prescribe hate for an enemy, the example of God's love for us—"while we were yet sinners" (Romans 5:8)—compels us to love our enemies. That doesn't mean that we don't stand up and fight people who persecute innocent people. But as we lay down our lives to defend the innocent, we do not wish hell even upon the violent oppressor. We pray for a change of heart in them, asking God to lead them to repentance and faith in Jesus Christ. Paul, the author of this passage, was once a violent oppressor of Christians. By praying for people like he did, we bless those who curse us.

The particular need of people who curse us is not curses, but blessing. Likewise, consider other people's needs in every circumstance. Is a woman rejoicing after a marriage proposal? Then rejoice with her from your heart. Is someone you know grieving a loss? Then go and sit with that person. Do not be quick to speak, but pray for a heart that shares the person's pain and shares with tears.

Be the kind of person who looks for agreement. Look to delight in points of agreement. Certain disagreements may require confrontation, especially doctrinal errors being taught in the church (Titus 1:9), but don't be the kind of person who is always edging for a fight.

Be humble enough to think nothing of associating with people that society deems to be of a lower class. Whether a person is rich or homeless should not matter to the Spirit-filled Christian. Both are worth the believer's time and attention. What matters is that they are people. They are the ones for whom Christ died.

Christians ought to be humble, especially with reference to wisdom. We have indeed become wise unto salvation (2 Timothy 3:15). But unless God's grace had sent the gospel to us and softened our hearts to believe it, we would never have arrived at this wisdom on our own. Like the Christian who looks down on the Jewish branches that have been cut off (Romans 11), we are foolish to look down on others who do not believe in Jesus. If we do, we forget who grafted us into the root. We forget from where we came.

In extreme examples where violent oppressors are murdering or assaulting innocents, there is a time for Christians to take part in just wars (Ecclesiastes 3:8). But in the case of interpersonal relationships, even if someone acts terrible toward the Christian, we are directed to not respond in like fashion. Even if someone slaps you on the cheek, turn the other one to him (Matthew 5:39). That doesn't mean that Christians shouldn't seek to escape danger, or even fight off an attack to get away, but it does mean that we do not personally bring justice to earth by executing the penalty that sinners deserve for their offenses against us. God will use government to carry out His judgments, and if a person escapes government, a final judgment day still awaits him or her. If a hateful person curses us, then don't respond in kind. Rather, turn away wrath with soft answers (Proverbs 15:1).

It is important to underscore that Christian peacemaking does not mean that there is never a time to fight. Ecclesiastes 3 says that there is a time for war and a time for peace, and this godly principle still applies to Christians. There is a difference between turning the other cheek and allowing the cheek of another person to continue to be struck. The innocent children who have fallen into the hands of terrorists need to be rescued and defended, not ignored or forgotten. Love for enemies is not about radical pacifism, but about the heart and motivations of a Christian.

41

Governments

*"Render to all what is due them: tax to whom tax is
due; custom to whom custom; fear to whom fear;
honor to whom honor"*

—*Romans 13:7*

Governments are meant to protect people and preserve peace. By and large, the governments of the world have performed this basic function. Even today in virtually every society on earth, if someone is wanting to commit murder, he must think twice on account of government. If he contemplates stealing, then he must consider whether or not he will get caught. Virtually every nation on earth throughout history has operated under a system of laws that restrain human evil. The reason for this phenomenon, Paul tells us in Romans 13:1-7, is that God's sovereign hand is behind the scenes orchestrating the governing authorities. Because of His sovereign establishment of government, Christians should live in subjection to it. We are not called to be political zealots who seek to overthrow authorities. We are called to pay taxes and be respectful to those in positions of political power.

13:1-7   Every person is to be in subjection to the governing
          authorities. For there is no authority except from God,

and those which exist are established by God. Therefore whoever resists authority has opposed the ordinance of God; and they who have opposed will receive condemnation upon themselves. For rulers are not a cause of fear for good behavior, but for evil. Do you want to have no fear of authority? Do what is good and you will have praise from the same; for it is a minister of God to you for good. But if you do what is evil, be afraid; for it does not bear the sword for nothing; for it is a minister of God, an avenger who brings wrath on the one who practices evil. Therefore it is necessary to be in subjection, not only because of wrath, but also for conscience' sake. For because of this you also pay taxes, for rulers are servants of God, devoting themselves to this very thing. Render to all what is due them, tax to whom tax is due; custom to whom custom; fear to whom fear; honor to whom honor.

Are there any exceptions to these rules? Of course there are. Even though it is generally true that God uses government to execute judgment against lawbreakers, sin still infects government. The problem of sin manifests in government in two ways. First, the individuals involved as governing authorities are individual sinners. Therefore they are prone to political corruption, thefts, lying, and every example of human sin. Individuals in authority sometimes use their power to hurt people. But individual sin does not mean that we should not respect the *office* of a governing authority.

Second, the general principle that governing authorities come from God does not mean that there is no such thing as an *illegitimate government*. That is to say, it is possible that an entire government can rise to power for a time in opposition to the righteous purpose for which God creates governments. God is sovereign over even this, since nothing can happen unless He at least allows it to happen. But in the same way that God allows sin to take place, but is never the Author of sin, God allows false governments to arise for a time, but is not the Source of these authorities. As difficult as it will be for Christians to understand at the time, He will work the actions of those governments together for good to His people (Romans 8:28), even as they operate for evil (Genesis 50:20).

When Paul wrote this thirteenth chapter of the book of Romans around 56 AD, Nero was the Emperor of Rome. At this point in history,

Nero was a decent ruler. He would only later become maniacal, behead Paul, burn Rome, blame Christians, and begin a war with Israel in 67 AD that would result in her complete destruction in 70 AD.

Paul's thirteenth chapter provides general principles for living under a peaceful government, but if rulers become tyrannical, God will overthrow them from within or use another government to topple an entire regime. God used several allies, including the United States of America, to overthrow the Nazi government of Germany. Likewise, the reign of the Islamic State will not be permanent. Once the evil of Nero's reign had reached its fill, God removed him from office. God did not cause Nero's reign of terror. He allowed it. In 68 AD, God allowed Nero to commit suicide. Similar to what happened under Nero, Christians would endure nine more great waves of persecution from Roman Emperors. Nero brought the first (64 AD), and the worst one was the last one under Diocletian/Galerius (303-311 AD). These finally ended when Constantine, who may have been a Christian, signed the Edict of Milan (313 AD), which prohibited persecution of Christians.

The general teaching about government (13:1-7) does not mean that Christians ought never to oppose, or even sometimes fight, an evil governing authority. An excellent case can be made that the tyranny of England that precipitated the American Revolution brought Americans into a just war. Likewise, to rebel against the governing authorities in the South during the Civil War was to fight for justice. In certain unique times in history, there comes a time to fight unjust governments, but the larger principle remains. It is necessary for Christians to be in subjection to governing authorities.

13:8-10   Owe nothing to anyone except to love one another; for he who loves his neighbor has fulfilled the law. For this, "YOU SHALL NOT COMMIT ADULTERY, YOU SHALL NOT MURDER, YOU SHALL NOT STEAL, YOU SHALL NOT COVET," and if there is any other commandment, it is summed up in this saying, "YOU SHALL LOVE YOUR NEIGHBOR AS YOURSELF." Love does no wrong to a neighbor; therefore love is the fulfillment of the law.

Paul now circles back around to the overarching principle that governs individual Christian behavior. This practical section of Christian principles (Romans 12-16) first of all described the entire Christian life as a spiritual act of worship (12:1-2). Then it assigned a context to where this life of worship is primarily lived out, namely the church (12:3-8). But the overarching principle of how we live our worshipful Christian lives in the church or in the world is *love*. The command "let love be without hypocrisy" (12:9) means that Christians need to love people sincerely. If we do that, not only will we have nothing to fear from government, but we will do well in every area of our Christian lives.

If our hearts are filled with love for our brothers, then the keeping of moral commands will come from the heart. Obedience will come *naturally*, as it were. We will not steal because we care about our brother and would not want to injure him by defrauding him. We will not look at pornography because we care about people, whose bodies are made for God and only given to the husband or wife to whom the person is meant to be given in marriage.

This section about obeying moral laws flows out of the previous passage about governing authorities. If we do right, we do not need to fear the punishment of governing authorities. If a driver is not speeding, he doesn't have to look ahead in the bushes for police cars. But more than that, if a Christian loves his neighbor as himself, he does not have to worry about breaking God's moral commandments. Far be it from the one who loves to hurt others.

42

Acceptance

"Now accept the one who is weak in faith, but not for the purpose of passing judgment on his opinions"

—*Romans 14:1*

Paul is ever the gospel preacher and never the moralist. He is teaching us to live by Christian principles. These include commands of things we have to do, like pay our taxes and be respectful to government. These also include prohibitions, like ones against adultery, murder, stealing, and coveting (an inward problem of the heart that may never even have an outward manifestation). Here now, Paul wants to ensure that Christians understand that we are not to indulge our flesh with excessive alcohol, with sex outside of marriage, or with that which feeds our carnal desires to fight. Paul outlaws these things, but not the way that governing authorities do. He doesn't list rules and punishments. Rather, he touches three areas of carnality with the conquering power of the gospel.

13:11-14   Do this, knowing the time, that it is already the hour for you to awaken from sleep; for now salvation is nearer to us than when we believed. The night is almost gone, and the day is near. Therefore let us lay aside the deeds of darkness and put on the armor of light. Let us behave properly as in the day, not in carousing and drunkenness, not in sexual promiscuity and sensuality, not in strife and jealousy. But put on the Lord Jesus Christ, and make no provision for the flesh in regard to its lusts.

Salvation is nearer today than it was on the day when Christ came into our hearts. Jesus already saved us from the *penalty* of our sins. "Having been justified through faith, we have peace with God through our Lord Jesus Christ" (Romans 5:1). But the attractive *power* of sin somehow still inexplicably creeps back up on us. This is our struggle while we remain in this world (Romans 7:14-25). But salvation is coming any day now. The very *presence* of sin will be utterly removed from us forever when Jesus comes back again. When will He return? We do not know, but Paul encourages us with the truism that the return of the King is one day closer today than it was yesterday! Since the metaphorical daylight of His coming is about to eliminate the darkness that is this tempting world, let's not act like creatures of the night. As we think about the second coming of Jesus, our minds and hearts become steadfast to resist temptation.

This call to look to the heavens for the return of Jesus is not motivated by rules and punishments. It is a gospel-driven appeal to the heart of the Christian. We are people who love the Lord Jesus Christ. So, let us "put on the Lord Jesus Christ," meaning that we should seek to contact Him in our minds and in our hearts. Instead of thinking of ways to satisfy the cravings of sinful flesh, think of ways to come into contact with Jesus Christ. Invite the filling of the Holy Spirit through prayer. Think about the propositions of Romans 6-8, and thus put on the mind of Christ. Our principled living is not motivated by keeping rules, but rather by loving Christ.

The overarching principle of love includes charitableness toward other Christians. It is sad that many Christians are quick to pick at other Christians over matters that are not weighty enough to demand confrontation. Paul has just given three examples of fleshly behaviors that are a big deal, things that have no place in the Christian community.

The **first**, drunken carousing, is the surrender of the body to the delights of the world. Worldly people find their only comfort in using drugs or alcohol to numb themselves to the pain of their real lives, pretending for a time that their lives are a party. In reality, unbelievers are under the wrath of God and destined for hell. Christians must not join in their partying and assist them in their self-delusion. Nor is it fitting for someone who has put on Christ to allow another to control him or her. If

Jesus is Lord, then how can a Christian surrender control of the body to a substance? Likewise, how can Christians give our bodies to sexual sin when our bodies are meant to be given to the Lord as a spiritual act of worship (12:1)? Sexual sin is therefore the **second** strong prohibition.

But the **third** prohibition of Romans 13:11-14 is actually the root sin that gives rise to so much division in the church. "Strife and jealousy" (13:13) is the fleshly desire to fight others and attain a feeling of significance or accomplishment by defeating or conquering others. The Christian life is meant to be lived in community (12:3-8). But instead of serving together, each Christian contributing to the body of Christ according to his or her spiritual gifts, in proportion to his or her faith, Christians often try to make themselves *look* like a contributing member of the church by rooting out problems they see in others. After all, if I can help to purify the church, that is to her benefit. But the problem is that "strife and jealousy" are the real motives behind many of these efforts for purity.

14:1-4   Now accept the one who is weak in faith, but not for the purpose of passing judgment on his opinions. One person has faith that he may eat all things, but he who is weak eats vegetables only. The one who eats is not to regard with contempt the one who does not eat, and the one who does not eat is not to judge the one who eats, for God has accepted him. Who are you to judge the servant of another? To his own master he stands or falls; and he will stand, for the Lord is able to make him stand.

At the time of the writing of Romans, the largely Gentile believers in Rome observed the Jewish background believers struggling to accept the freedom they had to eat anything. The Jewish believers were used to kosher rules, so it was hard for them to accept that there was nothing inherently wrong with pork, for example. Because Jewish-background believers who struggled with the findings of the Acts 15 council were not as strong in the faith as they ought to have been, one might assume that Paul would rebuke them for their lack of faith. But no! He rebukes those who criticize them.

The believer who struggles to eat formerly unclean foods is struggling in his faith, but this turns out to be a relatively minor problem. Paul does call them "weak in faith," but relative to the contentious spirit he sees in those who criticize them, the problem is negligible. The major issue is the strife caused by the picky Christian who has too much to say about other Christians' walk with God.

The picky Christian needs to accept his brother and stop being condescending about that minor point of weakness that he observes in his brother. It is only a speck of sawdust. Jesus warned about hypocritical divisiveness in the church; "Or how can you say to your brother, 'Let me take the speck out of your eye,' and behold, the log is in your own eye?" (Matthew 7:4). The strife-causing knit-picker needs to remember the words of the Lord and remember Whose servant his brother is. Our Christian brothers do not belong to us as our servants. Each of us belong to the Lord, so we are to give one another space to work things out between the Lord and His servant.

Ironically, as Paul rebukes certain Roman Christians for their contentiousness, Paul is helping them get a "speck" out of their eyes, which indicates that there is a time to rebuke other Christians. But Paul's point is founded upon the premise that there is a distinction between major and minor concerns. He will give some examples of minor concerns (things that ought to be overlooked) in the passage that follows. But drunkenness/carousing, sexual promiscuity/sensuality, and strife/jealousy are major concerns, since Paul judges Roman Christians for the latter. The church is the body of Christ (12:3-8), so those who stir up strife in the church are committing a major sin.

43

Liberty

"One person regards one day above another, another regards every day alike. Each person must be fully convinced in his own mind"

—Romans 14:5

It is striking that the thing from which Paul makes his appeal, the foundation point against which no one would argue, is that every believer engaged in the controversy that Paul is addressing is individually committed to the Lordship of Jesus Christ. These are not liberal, loose-living, hyper-grace, license-to-sin Christians. These are devoted followers of Jesus who are sincerely trying to live out their faith in a hostile world. This is a close community where people see what the others eat and do not eat. This is a zealous community where people care about what the Lord thinks about the behavior of everyone in their church. But do Christians have liberty to live according to their own conscience before God?

14:5-9   One person regards one day above another, another regards every day alike. Each person must be fully convinced in his own mind. He who observes the day, observes it for the Lord, and He who eats, does so for the Lord, for He gives thanks to God; and he who eats not, for the Lord he does not eat, and gives thanks to God. For not one of us lives for himself, and not one dies for himself; for if we live, we live for the Lord, or if we die, we die for the Lord; therefore whether we live or die, we are the Lord's. For to this end Christ died and lived again, that He might be Lord both of the dead and the living.

In verses 5 and 6, individual terms like "one," "another," "each," and "he" underscore that there are different individual opinions on a matter. But in verses 7 and 8, Paul uses "we" or "us" seven times. The point is that this is an in-house debate. It is okay with Paul that there be differences of opinion, but each believer needs to remember that in the end, it is not just him and the Lord who matter. Christ died to redeem "us" as His bride, so we all belong together to the Lord.

The issue of whether or not there are some days that are holier than others may have a right and a wrong side. But the issue itself is minor. What matters more is that the person is trying to be submissive to his Master in this regard. The issue of not eating certain foods, although it has a right position (the brother in 14:1 is called "weak"), is a minor issue. What matters is sincerely trying to submit to the will of the Master. Submission to Lordship and preserving the unity of the Spirit through the bond of peace (Ephesians 4:3) are major issues in the face of these minor differences of opinion.

44

Judging

*"Therefore let us not judge one another anymore, but
rather determine this—not to put an obstacle or a
stumbling block in a brother's way"*

—Romans 14:13

Paul dissuades judgmental believers from trying to enforce their
judgment about minor issues upon other believers. He has already
made the charge that some of the believers have contempt in their hearts,
are motivated by strife and jealousy, and are being judgmental as opposed
to making right judgments. Now he strengthens his prosecution by
reminding them about "the judgment seat of God." One of the things for
which we will have to give an account to God is the times in which we
stood haughtily in judgment over our brothers. In other words, to do so is a
grievous sin.

14:10-12   But you, why do you judge your brother? Or you
             again, why do you regard your brother with contempt?
             For we will all stand before the judgment seat of God.
             For it is written, "AS I LIVE, SAYS THE LORD,
             EVERY KNEE SHALL BOW TO ME, AND EVERY

TONGUE SHALL GIVE PRAISE TO GOD." So then each one of us will give an account of himself to God.

It is clear that Paul is addressing an in-house issue, and the use of language such as "your brother" indicates that Paul is not here questioning the salvation of anyone involved. "The judgment seat" (βῆμα, bema), which refers to an elevated place with steps leading up to it, is not the Great White Throne of Revelation 20:11-15. On that Judgment Day, everyone who appears before the Great White Throne without their name being written in the Lamb's Book of Life will be judged according to their works. Since "by the works of the law no flesh will be justified in His sight" (Romans 3:20), everyone judged by works will suffer "the second death, the lake of fire" (Revelation 20:14). But believers who approach the Great White Throne never get judged by works, because "another book was opened, which is the book of life" (20:12). "Therefore there is now no condemnation for those who are in Christ Jesus" (Romans 8:1).

Why then does Paul warn the divisive judgmental believers? He says, "each one of us will give an account of himself to God" (Romans 14:12). Remember that the final link in the Golden Chain of Redemption is *glorification*. The moment that the Christian spirit releases from the body (physical death), the believer is glorified, meaning that the presence of sin is entirely removed from the Christian. In that sense, the believer becomes *like* God. We will be forever sinless in heaven. This glorification happens immediately at death, because "to be absent from the body" (2 Corinthians 5:8) is "to be at home with the Lord."

The teaching about believers appearing before the *Bema* of Christ (Romans 14:10-12) evidently happens on "the day" (1 Corinthians 3:13) when we see him face to face and "know fully just as [we] also have been fully known" (1 Corinthians 13:12). When our spirit flies from earth to His Bema, Christ will open our eyes to the truth. In areas where we were deceived about our own behavior, "the day" will show forth the truth (1 Corinthians 3:13). Our dead works will be burned away right before our eyes, and no reward will be given for that portion of our service to Him. There are rewards in heaven (1 Corinthians 3:14), and these rewards can be lost on account of the kind of behavior for which Paul is rebuking certain divisive judgmental Christians in Rome. Romans 14:5-9 was about Lordship, and Romans 14:10-12 is about how the Lord (the Master) will regard our service to Him on the day when we meet Him at His throne.

14:13-18   Therefore let us not judge one another anymore, but rather determine this—not to put an obstacle or a

> stumbling block in a brother's way. I know and am convinced in the Lord Jesus that nothing is unclean in itself; but to him who thinks anything to be unclean, to him it is unclean. For if because of food your brother is hurt, you are no longer walking according to love. Do not destroy with your food him for whom Christ died. Therefore do not let what is for you a good thing be spoken of as evil; for the kingdom of God is not eating and drinking, but righteousness and peace and joy in the Holy Spirit. For he who in this way serves Christ is acceptable to God and approved by men.

The big-picture concluding exhortation of Romans 14 is for us "to not judge one another anymore." That does not mean that we are not to form judgments about sin or even to form them against Christians. That is precisely what Paul is doing in rebuking believers for causing strife (13:13) through their contemptuous attitudes (14:10). Paul addresses major issues, like drunkenness, sexual promiscuity, and jealousy (13:13). But there are minor differences of opinion that arise in the house of the Christian community, things genuine believers who are genuinely submitted to the Lordship of Christ genuinely disagree about. Believers must allow others to have their "own conviction before God" with regard to these things.

The postmodern spirit of the age is particularly disdainful of Christian judgments. They love passages like Romans 14:13, because it can be used as a club against Christians who uphold biblical morality, especially regarding sexual ethics. What they deliberately forget is that the context of the passage is not about sexual immorality, but is rather about the observation of certain holidays and the prohibition of certain foods and drink. Is there any way for us to know if sexual ethics can be grouped together with these issues and treated as the same kind of thing?

In Romans 1:24-27, sexual sins are used as the primary example of human idolatry. People are increasingly *given over* to sexual sins because they *exchange* the truth of God for a lie. That exchange can even devolve down to the point of *exchanging* natural sex between a husband and wife, where there is a complementary relationship, for unnatural sex with a mirror image of oneself, someone of the same gender. Homosexual behavior exchanges God's created design (a unifying act that has the potential to procreate) for the opposite (a damaging act that has no potential to procreate). Paul goes on to give twenty-one other examples of flagrant sin (Romans 1:28-32). Romans 2:1 adds judgmentalism to this list, because "in that which you judge another, you condemn yourself; for you who judge practice the same things." Paul underscores the universality of sin.

Then in Romans 2:4, Paul previews the gospel that will be fully revealed beginning in Romans 3:21. "Do you think lightly of the riches of his kindness and tolerance and patience . . ." It is as if God were reading the playbook of the secular humanists of postmodern America because He uses their favorite word: "tolerance." But to their dismay, Paul doesn't end the quotation there. He continues: ". . . not knowing that the kindness of God leads you to repentance?"

The gospel requires *repentance*. Those who stubbornly refuse to repent "are storing up wrath for [themselves] in the day of wrath and revelation of the righteous judgment of God" (Romans 2:5). They reject the gospel and will thus be judged by works (2:6), their names not written in the Lamb's Book of Life (Revelation 20:15). Those who accept the gospel (2:4) show forth that acceptance "by perseverance in doing good" (Romans 2:7).

Since the idea of a *Christian* who has *embraced* his or her sexual *immorality* is foreign to Paul, it is no wonder that he expresses indignation toward the Corinthians for *not* judging sexual immorality in their midst. "It is actually reported that there is immorality among you . . ." (1 Corinthians 5:1). Paul says that he has "already judged him who has so committed this" (5:3). He directs the Corinthians "not to associate with any so-called brother if he is an immoral person, or covetous, or an idolater, or a reviler, or a drunkard, or a swindler—not even to eat with such a one" (5:11). Paul will not grant that a person is truly a Christian just because he claims to be a "brother," if these major unrepentant sins are present in the person's life. Paul does not think that Christians no longer sin or struggle with sin (Romans 7:14-25), but if a person is embracing his or her sin, refusing to repent, then Paul assumes that they are not Christians.

What's more, Paul calls on Christians to make a right judgment against such a person. In the extreme case (such as the blatant unrepentant sexual immorality described in 1 Corinthians 5:1), the church may have to "remove the wicked man from among yourselves" (1 Corinthians 5:13). Later if the person repents as this Corinthian eventually did, the church "should rather forgive and comfort him, otherwise such a one might be overwhelmed by excessive sorrow" (2 Corinthians 2:7). "Do you not judge those who are within the Church?" (1 Corinthians 5:12)

Before Paul said so (Romans 14:13), Jesus taught, "Do not judge so that you will not be judged" (Matthew 7:1). Likewise before Paul said so (1 Corinthians 5:12), Jesus taught, "If your brother sins, go and show him his fault in private; if he listens to you, you have won your brother. But if he does not listen to you, take one or two more with you, so that BY THE MOUTH OF TWO OR THREE WITNESSES EVERY FACT MAY BE CONFIRMED. If he refuses to listen to them, tell it to the church; and if he refuses to listen even to the church, let him be to you as a Gentile and tax collector. Truly I say to you, whatever you bind on earth shall have been bound in heaven; and whatever you loose on earth shall have been loosed in heaven" (Matthew 18:15-18).

So, in the church, it is important for believers to form judgments. But these must be right judgments. They must not be mere differences of opinion as some of the Romans had about morally neutral issues such as observing holidays and abstaining from certain foods.

14:19-23   So then we pursue the things which make for peace and the building up of one another. Do not tear down the work of God for the sake of food. All things indeed are clean, but they are evil for the man who eats and gives offense. It is good not to eat meat or to drink wine, or to do anything by which your brother stumbles. The faith which you have, have as your own conviction before God. Happy is he who does not condemn himself in what he approves. But he who doubts is condemned if he eats, because his eating is not from faith; and whatever is not from faith is sin.

The point of Romans 14 is to call believers to be gracious toward one another. That does not mean tolerating sin, like the sins that the mirror exposed in Romans 1:18-3:20. It means leaving room for disagreement on points where the Bible does not provide a definitive word. Remember that the first-generation believers who lived in Rome did not have the Book of Acts (10:9-16, 15:19-29) to give a definitive word about some of their questions. They only had the Hebrew Bible. But Paul's letter came to Rome as authoritative Scripture (see comments on Romans 1:1).

As the New Testament canon was completed, we were not left with less revelation. We had a more definitive word from which to form judgments. The questions that faced the Romans (holidays and food) are not questions for us. We are free to eat and free to celebrate or to abstain as a free act of worship unto the Lord. We are free to disagree on things about which the Scripture has not spoken, but "happy is he who does not condemn himself in what he approves" (Romans 14:22).

45

Strength

"Now we who are strong ought to bear the weaknesses of those without strength and not just please ourselves"

—Romans 15:1

A strong Christian living in Rome in 56 AD when Paul's letter arrived was free to eat anything, free to drink anything, free to celebrate or not celebrate special holidays. But it would not be a sign of his strength to invite Jewish background believers to a party at his house, to roast a pig, and to rejoice with wine and singing on the night of the Passover. The Jewish Christian would in fact be free to eat, free to drink, and free not to observe Passover traditions in his own home that night. But the strong believer who understood this also understood that his Jewish Christian friend might be struggling with these issues. We learn from Romans 15:1-6 that it is not a sign of strength when a strong Christian tries to force other believers to see the truth of a matter, when that matter is not urgent and when the other believer could actually be pushed away from Christ through the strong believer's pushing of the issue.

15:1-6   Now we who are strong ought to bear the weaknesses
           of those without strength and not just please ourselves.
           Each of us is to please his neighbor for his good, to his

edification. For even Christ did not please Himself; but as it is written, "THE REPROACHES OF THOSE WHO REPROACHED YOU FELL ON ME." For whatever was written in earlier times was written for our instruction, so that through perseverance and the encouragement of the Scriptures we might have hope. Now may the God who gives perseverance and encouragement grant you to be of the same mind with one another according to Christ Jesus, so that with one accord you may with one voice glorify the God and Father of our Lord Jesus Christ.

Notice from the first verse of chapter 15 that there is a right and a wrong side of these issues. Paul is not pushing an early version of postmodernism, where each person defines what is true for him or her. Rather, struggling to feel free from the Law is called "the weakness of those without strength." "Weakness" here does not refer to feeble arms, but to being feeble in the faith. These are believers who stand upon the Truth, but they are still unsteady, still not steadfast (Galatians 2:6-8) in the Faith once for all handed down to us (Jude 1:3).

The strong believer here in Romans 15:1-6 is not just the person who is strong in faith, but also the person who is strong in love. He has greater understanding of doctrine than some other believers do. He walks in that truth, living by faith, not by sight. But he also genuinely cares for other believers. He charts a course in his interactions with weaker believers. That course is never to show himself stronger than them, but always to help them along in their walk with God. He does what the Lord leads him to do, things that will encourage faith in weaker believers.

Christ is the perfect example of the strong. Although perfectly morally righteous, He did not parade his righteousness. He refused to wear a phylactery on his forehead. He didn't wear a long flowing robe. He didn't make pious prayers standing on street corners. He didn't throw money into the offering in front of people to be seen by them. So little did He parade his righteousness that the Pharisees were convinced that He wasn't righteous.

They condemned Him for eating with tax collectors and sinners and for healing on the Sabbath. The reproaches of those who reproach the Father fell upon the Son. But Jesus didn't care about looking good in the eyes of others. He cared about being good, and the reality was that there was no good teacher besides Him (Mark 10:17). He didn't care about being good at teaching, and it wasn't enough that what He taught was good. What made Jesus so strong is that He cared about the weak, and He was willing to bear their reproaches in order to show them true strength that one day they also might be counted among the strong (Isaiah 53:12).

Strong Christians do not parade their righteousness. Rather, they humbly and prayerfully consider ways to edify other Christians, to make them stronger. Strong Christians are truly concerned about the strength of the church, not having one's own name regarded as strong. Too often believers look for ways to be regarded by others as being spiritual. One way to do that is by calling out the weaknesses of others. But love for the weaker brother means always trying to cover over weaknesses (1 Peter 4:8). As discussed in the comments of 14:13-23, that does not mean that we do not address sin. But it means that as much as possible, we seek to preserve the reputation of the sinner.

We don't draw attention to other believer's faults or to our strengths. We go to a sinning believer one on one first and only involve others when more private options fail (Matthew 18:15-17). The bottom line is that the strong will not be looking to be seen as strong, they "will genuinely be concerned" (Philippians 2:20) for the welfare of others.

46

Unity

*"Therefore, accept one another, just as Christ
also accepted us to the glory of God"*

—Romans 15:7

The final practical principle for Christian living is the importance of
Christian unity. John 17 is the longest prayer of Jesus that we have
recorded for us in Scripture. This high-priestly prayer is supremely
concerned about how Christians love one another and remain unified as we
serve the Lord together. Jesus offered this prayer just before He died and
rose again. Christian unity is obviously important to Jesus.

15:7-13   Therefore accept one another, just as Christ also accepted us
           to the glory of God. For I say that Christ has become a
           servant to the circumcision on behalf of the truth of God to
           confirm the promises given to the fathers, and for the
           Gentiles to glorify God for His mercy; as it is written,
           "THEREFORE I WILL GIVE PRAISE TO YOU
           AMONG THE GENTILES, AND I WILL SING TO
           YOUR NAME." Again he says, "REJOCE, O GENTILES,
           WITH HIS PEOPLE." And again, "PRAISE THE LORD
           ALL YOU GENTILES, AND LET ALL THE PEOPLES

PRAISE HIM." Again Isaiah says, "THERE SHALL COME THE ROOT OF JESSEE, AND HE WHO ARISES TO RULE OVER THE GENTILES, IN HIM SHALL THE GENTILES HOPE."

The biggest hindrance to unity among the early believers who lived in Rome was the rift between Gentile believers and Jewish believers. The Jewish believers would have been the ones who struggled with the idea of eating foods that were formerly considered unclean. They would have struggled with regarding "every day alike," since three of the Jewish festivals had been mandatory.

The cross is the remedy to disunity. In the book of Ephesians, Paul speaks of the unity that was provided by Jesus' death on the cross. "For He Himself is our peace, who made both groups into one and broke down the barrier of the dividing wall, by abolishing in His flesh the enmity, which is the Law of commandments contained in ordinances, so that in Himself He might make the two into one new man, thus establishing peace, and might reconcile them both in one body through the cross, by it having put to death the enmity" (Ephesians 2:14-16).

In Romans 15:7-13, Paul quotes from the Old Testament four times. Each passage underscores the same reality. The Gentiles are welcome at God's table. If the Jews in Rome could learn to accept even those whom they once considered Gentile dogs, then surely no racial barriers need to separate us today. The church is the most global institution on the planet. There are probably as many genuine Christians in China today as there are in the United States of America.

The strong Christian is the one who is like Christ. The prayer of the strong is the one that agrees with Jesus' high priestly prayer. Seeing it answered calls for selflessness on the part of individual Christians. When we truly seek to glorify God, we do not please ourselves. We live and we pray for unity within the body of Christ. "Now may the God who gives perseverance and encouragement grant you to be of the same mind with one another according to Christ Jesus, so that with one accord you may with one voice glorify the God and Father of our Lord Jesus Christ" (Romans 15:5).

SECTION 7

Good News Going Forward
Romans 15:14-16:27

47

Arriving

*"in the power of signs and wonders, in the power of the Spirit;
so that from Jerusalem and round about as far as Illyricum I
have fully preached the gospel of Christ"*

—*Romans 15:19*

We are arriving at the destination. When Romans 1:18-3:20 first located us on the map, we were dead men walking, lost in a jungle of sin. "But now" (Romans 3:21), the righteousness of God has manifested to us. We were justified right where we stood when we believed in Jesus Christ (3:21-5:21).

The waters of baptism then gave us a vision of the new people that we became when we trusted in Christ (6:1-11). We must count ourselves dead to sin and alive to Christ. Although we may stumble, we learn to walk in the Spirit, knowing that as His adopted children, we are forever secure in His love (6-8).

Before going anywhere, we turned our eyes to heaven and saw a glimpse of how powerful God's hand really is. He is sovereign over the hearts of men and the course of nations, Israel being central to His plan (9-11).

Then God set us to walking, telling us what principles we are to observe as we go (12:1-15:13). It was the gospel that led us every step of the way so far, and we must continue to look to the good news as we go forward from here.

Romans 15:14-16:27 brings Paul's letter to a close and us to our destination. We are aware that one day we will be glorified with God in heaven. The very presence of sin will forever be removed from us, and we will dwell in the presence of God forever. That is the last link in the Golden Chain of Redemption (8:29-30). But Paul's letter leaves us here in the jungle of sin, right where we are supposed to be at the present time. The destination of the Romans Road is at the ends of the earth, wherever each of us are today, and especially wherever the gospel has not yet taken root. The destination of the Romans Road is wherever a strong Christian stands.

The point of the letter is to establish us in the gospel. Some of us got saved for the first time by reading this book. Perhaps Romans 3:23-25 revealed the manifold beauty of the gospel to you for the first time. The light burst into your soul. Your heart understood the gospel of the glory of God. You saw the glory that is in the face of Christ (2 Corinthians 4:4).

Perhaps you came to Romans as a believer, but unsteady in your walk with Christ. You knew Him, but your faith was weak. Maybe the dangers of this world make you feel insecure, and the security of being a child of God (Romans 8) was what you most desperately needed to see. Maybe you needed a higher view of God's sovereignty (Romans 9-11) in order to really trust God and rest in Him. Maybe you just needed some course corrections, adjustments to the principles by which you live your life (12:1-15:13), to really live like the Christian that you are. However you came to Romans, the road brings you out at a better destination. God uses Romans to make Christians and to make Christians *strong*.

One of the great miracles of the Christian life is that sanctification never ends until we are glorified in God's presence. That is, we will continually be undergoing a process of being made into the image of Christ until the day we die or Christ comes back to get us. There is an ongoing process whereby He works His will into our character and sinfulness out of our character. His Word is the tool that He uses to transform us (12:1). The Holy Spirit is the One who wields the tool (8:1-4). As we encounter the Word, that Word in our minds and hearts becomes a handle that is taken hold of by the Holy Spirit. He uses the Word that we hear to build faith (10:17). As we live by faith (remember the thesis of Paul's letter to the Romans in 1:17: "the just shall live by faith"), the Spirit is at work in our hearts, changing our hearts "to will and to work for His good pleasure" (Philippians 2:13). So every time we return to the Word of God, it has a destination to which it will bring us.

Paul now draws his letter to a close. As the reader completes his tour through Romans, he is either a Christian or he is not. There are no degrees of spiritual birth (John 3:3). Either a person has the new birth or he does not. If he does not, then there is a particular urgency to return to the beginning of the book and pray for eyes to see the truth.

The tour through Romans is ending. If the reader is a Christian, then the Word of God recorded in Romans has not returned void (Isaiah 55:11), but has further sanctified the reader. As Paul draws his letter to a close, take it in carefully, to give handle to the Holy Spirit. Let Him put a seal on the work He has done in you as He brought you through the book of Romans, just as when He sealed your soul for salvation on the day you heard and believed the gospel for the first time (Ephesians 1:13-14).

The "revelation of the secret mystery" is the uncovering of the gospel. Having eyes to see Jesus is the meaning of life (Philippians 3:8). To see Him is to know Him, and to know Him more is to be made like Him. To be with Him is the ultimate destination, but Romans opens spiritual eyes even now. We are the Romans who received this letter, the friends of Paul who imitate Paul as he imitates Christ. Let this trip through Romans finish its work. It reveals the secret mystery, so let us keep gazing at the One Romans makes known.

15:14-17   And concerning you, my brethren, I myself also am convinced that you yourselves are full of goodness, filled with all knowledge and able also to admonish one another. But I have written very boldly to you on some points so as to remind you again, because of the grace that was given me from God, to be a minister of Christ Jesus to the Gentiles, ministering as a priest the gospel of God, so that my offering of the Gentiles may become acceptable, sanctified by the Holy Spirit. Therefore in Christ Jesus I have found reason for boasting in things pertaining to God.

The Roman Christians who received Paul's letter became more like Paul when they read it. But Paul's life was hidden in Christ (Colossians 3:3). Paul's only boast was Christ in him (Galatians 6:14). That Christ lived inside of Paul was Paul's only hope of glory (Colossians 1:27). God made Paul to be an example for all believers to imitate, presumably because of all sinful people, Paul imitated Christ more than anyone else. So, the repeated commands to imitate Paul (Philippians 3:17, 1 Corinthians 4:16, 11:1) are the condescension of God to change us from what we really were—each of us a "chief of sinners" (1 Timothy 1:15)—to what we are to become—"slaves of Christ Jesus" (Romans 1:1). We like the Romans look to Paul's example as we strive toward the destination of becoming like Christ.

The church at Rome was filled with believers who were already somewhat strong. They were "full of goodness, filled with all knowledge and able also to admonish one another." But Paul still wanted them to be "sanctified by the Holy Spirit." Paul's greatest desire was not to make a great name for himself, but rather to offer something acceptable to the Lord he loves. The Gentiles in particular were responding to Paul's preaching. He wanted them not only to be saved, but also to be holy, set apart for God.

Part of being holy, set apart to God, is being set apart for the gospel. That is how Paul introduced himself in the first verse (1:1). Now we get to see what that looks like in Paul's heart. We see that Paul is motivated by the thought of pleasing God and bringing glory to His name. Where it is evident that Christ Himself is at work more than the merely human efforts of men like Paul, all the glory goes to Jesus.

15:18-21   For I will not presume to speak of anything except what Christ has accomplished through me, resulting in the obedience of the Gentiles by word and deed, in the power of signs and wonders, in the power of the Spirit; so that from Jerusalem and round about as far as Illyricum I have fully preached the gospel of Christ. And thus I aspired to preach the gospel, not where Christ was already named, so that I would not build on another man's foundation; but as it is written, "THEY WHO HAD NO NEWS OF HIM SHALL SEE, AND THEY WHO HAVE NOT HEARD SHALL UNDERSTAND."

Paul mentions three ways in which Jesus receives glory through Paul's ministry. **First**, Jesus is honored when the Gentiles come to obey God (Romans 1:5), not only in word, but also in deed (15:18). **Second**, Jesus is glorified when the preaching of the gospel is accompanied by signs and wonders (15:19). Supernatural occurrences cannot be attributed to man. When done in the name of Jesus (Acts 4:10), miracles glorify that name. **Third**, when the gospel advances mightily in that name (Acts 4:12), it is evident that the Holy Spirit is empowering the ministry (Romans 15:19). Paul can say that the gospel has advanced "from Jerusalem and round about as far as Illyricum" (15:19) to the glory of the name of Jesus. The distance between the farthest point in Illyricum and Jerusalem was about fourteen hundred miles. Paul didn't evangelize in a straight line between them, but on three major journeys, each lasting years, he moved "round about" the region. Jesus was glorified by the gospel advance throughout that entire region.

The destination to which Romans brings us includes becoming a "minister" (λειτουργός, leitourgos). The root (leitos), from which the word for "minister" derives, meant "belonging to the people." It usually referred to a public servant in some official capacity. Someone in a public office was a "minister" of the State. But Paul "ministered as a priest" (ἱερουργέω, hierourgeó). He *ministered in holy things*. The strong Christian is someone who serves the public. More than simply a social worker, he has become a minister to bring "the gospel of God" to the public. If a person sees himself dead in sin (1:18-3:20), sees the gospel manifested (3:21-5:21), sees himself alive in Christ (6-8), sees God sovereign over all (9-11), and sees the principles of godly living (12:1-15:13), then he will soon see himself as a minister of the gospel (15:16). The gospel will have taken over his vision. His purpose in life will be to minister the gospel to others until the Lord brings him home.

48

Support

*"Now I urge you, brethren, by our Lord Jesus Christ and
by the love of the Spirit, to strive together with me in
your prayers to God for me"*

—Romans 15:30

At the outset of our journey through the book of Romans we saw that Paul prayed unceasingly for the Roman church. Paul's prayers moved from celebration to supplication, which is a model for us. Now as we near the end of our journey, we hear Paul calling the Roman believers to the same kind of prayer. Just as Paul prayed unceasingly (1:9), so now he urges the Romans to not only pray but to *strive* (15:30) in prayer. Paul's prayers were sure to receive a powerful answer from God, but how much more so will God answer prayer when many of His children join together in asking the same thing of Him? The Roman believers are arriving at the destination to which Paul hoped to bring them when he wrote his epistle to them. They are learning to pray. They are learning to intercede—to come between a circumstance and an omnipotent God and to stay there until God moves the circumstance.

Intercessory prayer is the primary support that Christians need to give to one another. Just as Paul was separated from the Romans by many miles and yet connected with them through prayer, so we also are able to pray for our brothers and sisters wherever they are in the world. In addition to prayer, there are also physical ways that believers can support one another.

15:22-29   For this reason I have often been prevented from coming to you; but now, with no further place for me in these regions, and since I have had for many years a longing to come to you whenever I go to Spain—for I hope to see you in passing, and to be helped on my way there by you, when I have first enjoyed your company for a while—but now, I am going to Jerusalem serving the saints. For Macedonia and Achaia have been pleased to make a contribution for the poor among the saints in Jerusalem. Yes, they were pleased to do so, and they are indebted to them. For if the Gentiles have shared in their spiritual things, they are indebted to minister to them also in material things. Therefore, when I have finished this, and have put my seal on this fruit of theirs, I will go on by way of you to Spain. I know that when I come to you, I will come in the fullness of the blessing of Christ.

Paul unabashedly raises financial support for the ministry. There are two causes that he seeks to fund. First, the Jewish believers in Jerusalem were the first to accept the Christ and have now become the biggest target for persecution by the Jewish people who do not believe in Jesus. It was difficult for the believers to participate in the economy, since they were ostracized. Paul seeks to help them by sending finances to them.

Second, Paul seeks to fund his own effort to bring the gospel to Spain. Paul was willing to suffer from a lack of material things, but it takes resources to accomplish big things. For starters, Paul would need to pay to board a ship to Spain, pay for food and water, and possibly pay some rent for a room in Spain. Both of Paul's causes were worthy of financial support.

The Roman Christians were committed to the cause of Christ, so they were probably happy to give support. In any case, Paul tells of the generosity of the believers from Macedonia and Achaia in order to inspire the believers from Rome to likewise give their financial support.

15:30-33   Now I urge you, brethren, by our Lord Jesus Christ and by the love of the Spirit, to strive together with me in your prayers to God for me, that I may be rescued from those who are disobedient in Judea, and that my service for Jerusalem may prove acceptable to the saints; so that I may come to you in joy by the will of God and find refreshing rest in your company. Now the God of peace be with you all. Amen.

Even ministers need the ministry of others. Although Paul desperately wants to get to Rome in order to minister the gospel there, "that I may obtain some fruit among you also, even as among the rest of the Gentiles" (Romans 1:13), he desperately needs the ministry of the Roman believers in order for it to happen. It is no small thing for Paul to make it to Rome. God will have to open some closed doors. First of all, when he goes down to Judea (he is probably in Corinth, Greece, as he writes the letter to the Romans), he knows that there are many Jews there who are very actively seeking to kill him. He needs God to protect his life. Second, he needs to minister in Jerusalem, complete that ministry, and receive a healthy send off from there. Third, he needs to travel fourteen hundred miles across the Mediterranean Sea from Jerusalem to Rome.

We know from Dr. Luke's account (Acts 21-28) that Paul does actually make it. In accordance with the prophecy given by Agabus (Acts 21:10-11), Paul is accosted by the Jews in Jerusalem and taken prisoner by the Romans. After a long wait and after appealing to Caesar, Paul is finally sent to Rome. The first ship he sails on does not make it. Paul endures shipwreck and snakebite, but eventually he appears before the emperor, just as Jesus said when Jesus first appeared to him (Acts 9:15).

Even as Romans 9-11 presents God perfectly bringing His will to pass, even as humans make decisions according to their own wills, it was God's will and therefore inevitable that Paul would make it to Rome, and yet the prayers of the Romans were instrumental. Paul knows that God is sovereign, and yet he *urges*, almost begs, for the Romans to pray him safely in to them. He increases the urgency of his request with the phrases "by our Lord Jesus Christ and by the love of the Spirit." Paul leans on the Romans to *really* pray because prayer really matters.

49

Partners

*"who for my life risked their own necks, to whom not only do
I give thanks, but also all the churches of the Gentiles"*

—*Romans 16:4*

Paul wrote his "Epistle to the Romans" to real people, many of whom he knew personally. Today we call Paul's letter "the book of Romans." It is read daily all over the world. But although the original recipients would have been glad to see that their old friend Paul had remembered their names, they would have had no idea that two thousand years later, their names would be remembered all over the world. In their time, they were obscure, just a few of Paul's many partners in the gospel. But their lives still matter today. In the same way, most of us who partner in the work of the gospel do so in obscurity, but we have no idea how our partnership will resonate for all eternity. Because the gospel matters for all eternity, we who partner in the gospel also matter for all eternity.

16:1-2   I commend to you our sister Phoebe, who is a servant of the church which is at Cenchrea; that you receive her in the Lord in a manner worthy of the saints, and that you help her in whatever matter she may have need of you; for she herself has also been a helper of many, and of myself as well.

It is interesting that Paul opens the last chapter of Romans speaking of a female servant of the Lord. Since the destination of the Romans Road is that we would become strong, sin-conquering, Spirit-filled ministers of the gospel, the commendation of Phoebe underscores the reality that Romans is written to Jew and Gentile, male and female alike. Does that mean that women can be ministers? It doesn't speak to women exercising authority over men in the church, as in becoming elder/overseers of the church (1 Timothy 2:12 forbids this), but it does mean that women can minister.

Phoebe obviously had an important ministry to carry out. Many believe that the implication of these verses is that she was selected to be the one to bring Paul's letter to Rome. Since she is commended to them and they are to "receive her," it is clear that she was actually being sent in person to them. Since they are to "help her in whatever matter she may have need of you," it is clear that she has some mission to accomplish in Rome. Paul wants the Romans to support her ministry among them. He recommends her for ministry on the basis of her previous track record, part of which was a benefit to Paul's ministry. She is clearly regarded as an equal partner in the gospel. It could very well be that Paul entrusted the letter that would change the world into her care to deliver it to the church in Rome.

16:3-16   Greet Prisca and Aquila, my fellow workers in Christ Jesus, who for my life risked their own necks, to whom not only do I give thanks, but also all the churches of the Gentiles; also greet the church that is in their house. Greet Epaenetus, my beloved, who is the first convert to Christ from Asia. Greet Mary, who has worked hard for you. Greet Adronicus and Junias, my kinsmen and my fellow prisoners, who are outstanding among the apostles, who also were in Christ before me. Greet Ampliatus, my beloved in the Lord. Greet Urbanus, our fellow worker in Christ, and Stachys my beloved. Greet Apelles, the approved in Christ. Greet those who are of the household of Aristobulus. Greet Herodian, my kinsman. Greet those of the household of Narcissus, who are in the Lord. Greet Tryphaena and Tryphosa, workers in the Lord.

Greet Persis the beloved, who has worked hard in the Lord. Greet Rufus, a choice man in the Lord, also his mother and mine. Greet Asycritus, Phlegon, Hermes, Patrobas, Hermas and the brethren with them. Greet Philologus and Julia, Nereus and his sister, and Olympas, and all the saints who are with them. Greet one another with a holy kiss. All the churches of Christ greet you.

The list of people Paul greets here is remarkable. Many of them would be worthy of study. But for our purposes, we will take note of the big picture. **First**, it is remarkable that Paul would endeavor to list the names of the actual people in the church at Rome that he personally knew. It shows that their names and faces had not faded from his memory. Some of us would perhaps shy away from listing names, being worried about missing people and hurting feelings. But Paul charges in headlong, a decision that can only be explained by Paul's active prayer life. Paul may have been separated from his friends by distance and years, but the truth of the claim he made with God as his witness "as to how unceasingly I make mention of you" (Romans 1:9) is now proven by his ability to remember their names.

Second, it is worth noting that the heat of battle forges the deepest relationships. These are people who have "risked their own necks" for Paul and he has risked his own for them in the ministry battle. If someone has been raised in a largely Christian country, it is easy to forget that the Christian life, especially when engaged in the Christian mission, is a battle. Satan is a real enemy. The world is largely conformed into his image. Human flesh is bent toward evil. To stand against these three enemies and to take ground against them for the Kingdom of God is a sure recipe for battle. But to stand together with a band of brothers, united under the banner of the Name, united by the cleansing power of Jesus' blood, united in drinking from the same Spirit, is to become one. Paul isn't just writing to some old friends. He is writing to his brothers and sisters in arms.

Finally, Paul's affection for these people bleeds from the page. He calls someone "beloved" four times. He calls some "kinsmen" as if they were actually blood relatives. He probably meant it as a term of endearment. Likewise, he calls one of the older women his "mother." He speaks of "brethren." He compliments one as a "choice man," another as "outstanding," another as "approved." He commends someone's hospitality. He repeatedly recognizes "hard work" and "fellow workers." He calls them all "saints." He doesn't want them to just casually greet each other. Following a cultural form, he calls for a "holy kiss," meaning that he wants them to express the kind of love to each other that he feels for each of them. These are his fellow soldiers, but even more, these are his own family.

50

Teachers

*"For the report of your obedience has reached to all; therefore
I am rejoicing over you, but I want you to be wise in what
is good and innocent in what is evil"*

—*Romans 16:19*

Paul's warning at the end of Romans is not unusual. Wherever Paul went, he knew that persecution awaited him, and he was ready to die there if need be. He knew he might never again visit a given church, so he wanted to leave them capable of standing on their own. He might never come back to set the house in order. Before Paul sailed for Jerusalem, knowing that he would never again return to Ephesus, he gathered the Ephesian elders and wept with them on the beach. He warned them that "savage wolves will come in among you, not sparing the flock" (Acts 20:29). These wolves would be false teachers who would pervert the Word of God that Paul had brought them.

16:17-20   Now I urge you, brethren, keep your eye on those who cause dissensions and hindrances contrary to the teaching which you learned, and turn away from them. For such men are slaves, not of the Lord Christ but of their own appetites; and by their smooth and flattering speech they

> deceive the hearts of the unsuspecting. For the report of your obedience has reached to all; therefore I am rejoicing over you, but I want you to be wise in what is good and innocent in what is evil. The God of peace will soon crush Satan under your feet. The grace of our Lord Jesus be with you.

Still today, false teachers within the church are the greatest danger that the church faces. If enemies of the cross who do not claim to believe that Jesus died on the cross and rose from the dead (Surah 4:157 of the Qur'an puts Muslims in that camp) spill the blood of Christians, then the blood of the martyrs will only be the seed of the church. From the ten waves of Roman persecution to today's persecuted house church in China to the Christians being killed by Islamic extremists, the gates of hell cannot resist the church (Matthew 16:18). But false teachers who disguise themselves, being called "Christian" but not truly knowing Christ, damage the church from within.

Paul urges the church at Rome to be on guard, as we must also be today. "But I am afraid that as the serpent deceived Eve by his craftiness, your minds will be led astray from the simplicity and purity of devotion to Christ. For if one comes and preaches another Jesus whom we have not preached, or you receive a different spirit which you have not received, or a different gospel which you have not accepted" (2 Corinthians 11:3-4a), we must recognize them, expose them, and reject them.

Around 1830 AD, Joseph Smith came preaching "another Jesus," one who was the spirit brother of Satan. Smith was animated by a "different spirit"—an unholy spirit of deception. He preached a "different gospel"—actually rewriting the words of Romans 4:5 to say the exact opposite of what the text actually says. The church must identify the Joseph Smiths of the world for who they are. Among the hundreds of millions of genuine believers on the planet, there are many million who claim the name of Jesus but actually follow another Jesus, have a different spirit and do not have the gospel. The genuine gospel, as found here in the book of Romans, is the standard by which every deviating teacher is exposed.

Paul is worried about this danger, so he reminds the believers to be both wise and innocent. They must themselves remain innocent of strange teachings, protecting their hearts. They must at the same time be expecting those teachers to come. They must be vigilant to keep them out of classrooms, away from their children, away from the pulpit. Elders have the special responsibility of guarding the doctrine of the church (Titus 1:9).

Paul is worried, but not overcome with it. In the end, he is still "rejoicing over [them]" and assures them that "the God of peace will soon crush Satan under [their] feet." God will empower the genuine believers for victory, but it is their "feet" (them being the instruments) that will overcome the false teachers whom Satan is animating. Paul speaks a blessing of "grace" over them, and grace will truly bring us home as well.

16:21-24   Timothy my fellow worker greets you, and so do Lucius and Jason and Sosipater, my kinsmen. I Tertius, who write this letter, greet you in the Lord. Gaius, host to me and to the whole church, greets you. Erastsus, the city treasurer greets you, and Quartus, the brother. [The grace of our Lord Jesus Christ be with you all. Amen.]

Paul was a juggernaut who crushed the enemy under his feet wherever he went, but Paul didn't go alone. On his first mission trip, he set out with Barnabas, taking John Mark as well. On the second trip, Paul went with Silas and soon picked up Timothy. There were also various other traveling companions who ministered along with Paul in many of the places Paul went. Luke probably joined Paul in Acts 16:11, where he (the author of the book of Acts) starts referring to Paul's mission team as "we" instead of "they." In contrast to the false teachers of which Paul warned, these ministers were faithful teachers of the same gospel that Paul received by direct revelation from Jesus Christ.

Timothy is an especially noteworthy servant who ministered alongside of Paul. Paul's complimentary description of him in Philippians 2:19-23 could not have been stronger. Two of Paul's epistles to him made it into the New Testament. As Paul writes the Romans, probably from Corinth, Timothy is right there by Paul's side. They may have been sitting right there together in Gaius' house when Paul wrote Romans, since the place where they met on Sundays was also a house where Paul slept. But Paul did not write with his own hand. One can picture him pacing back and forth or kneeling as he dictated the words that flowed from deep inside his heart. Perhaps Lucius, Jason, Sosipater, Quartus, Erastus, and Gaius were within earshot of the dictation and prayed in the Spirit as they heard the Word of God coming forth. Tertius, no doubt an educated man able to write clearly, quickly and carefully, captured the words that poured out of Paul. As it was in Corinth when the book of Romans was written and given to the world, so it is today that the church serves together and grows as each member does his or her part. We are the body of Christ.

Conclusion

"Now to Him who is able to establish you according to my gospel and the preaching of Jesus Christ, according to the revelation of the mystery which has been kept secret for long ages past"

—Romans 16:25

The purpose of Romans now becomes the conclusion of the book expressed as a prayer. It is God alone who is "able to establish you." That is the destination of Romans—that we the readers would be strong and firm in the Faith.

16:25-27   Now to Him who is able to establish you according to my gospel and the preaching of Jesus Christ, according to the revelation of the mystery which has been kept secret for long ages past, but now is manifested, and by the Scriptures of the prophets, according to the commandment of the eternal God, has been made known to all the nations, leading to obedience of faith; to the only wise God, through Jesus Christ, be the glory forever. Amen.

Christians are born by "my gospel," that is, the gospel Paul preached that he received by direct revelation from Jesus Christ. Nowadays many so-called Christians like to say that the gospel refers to a great many pieces of good news, virtually any news that anyone thinks is good to them. But Paul's gospel is not one among many. It is *the* gospel

(Galatians 1:7). Paul was set apart even from his mother's womb for this very purpose (Galatians 1:15), to receive directly from God the gospel as God defines it and deliver that gospel to the Gentiles, thus establishing the message once and for all. The book of Romans is the clear comprehensive statement of what that message is.

We have seen that Romans has seven sections, just like the seven hills of the city of Rome. We have now traversed those seven sections, and if our eyes have been opened, the gospel is now clearer to us than ever before.

The **first** section gives us an overview of where the book of Romans intends to take us. The destination is to become a free and willing slave (doulos) of Jesus Christ. Paul's life of prayer and unashamed proclamation of the gospel is a model for us. But getting there requires moving "from faith to faith" because "the just shall live by faith."

The **second** section locates us on the map. It pulls no punches. We learned that we are desperately wicked. Our hearts are idol factories. We exchange the glory of the incorruptible God for that which we can manufacture. God, in turn, gives us over to our idols and stores up judgment for a day of wrath.

The **third** section manifests the glorious good news of the gospel. God made a one-time sacrifice, publicly displaying His Son and pouring out wrath upon Him in order to demonstrate justice. This "propitiation" in Christ's blood paid the debt of sin in full. As a result, those sinners who look to Jesus Christ are counted to be righteous right where we stand. Sinners are justified by faith.

The **fourth** section reveals what changed in the sinner who received justification. The waters of baptism provide a reflection of a new creation. Old sinful patterns are broken and godly patterns take over. The believer still sins and will sometimes feel conflicted. But Christians are loved children of God and more than conquerors.

The **fifth** section takes the believer behind the scenes of this world to observe the work of the Director. We need to understand that God is sovereign over all. If we know that His providence dictates or allows everything that happens on earth and we know that He loves us, then we can trust Him no matter what. Israel belongs to God as His children, so as we consider Israel's past, present, and future, we become confident in our Father's plan. It is beyond our tracing out, but clearly a reason for us to rejoice.

The **sixth** section finally provides us with a list of principles for us to observe. It took a long time to get us to the point where we are ready to receive commands. If these are given too early, we may think that our work somehow contributes to our salvation. But once we understand grace, we do need to know how to conduct ourselves in this world. Our entire lives are to be given over to God as worship. We devote ourselves to participate in the local church, love well, obey authorities, walk in liberty, judge not, accept one another, exhibit true strength, and preserve unity.

The **seventh** and final section brings us to our arrival as devoted servants of Christ who support one another in ministry and pray unceasingly. We are on our way to Spain or to whatever unreached corner of the world the Lord has for us. The gospel that saved us has become our mission. The good news keeps going forward.

Now that the gospel has been revealed, it is no longer a mystery as we may think of the term. It is something previously hidden that has now been made known. The secret has been revealed. In a word, it is *Jesus*. In a book, it is *Romans*.

For long ages past, prophets spoke of the gospel, but only in types, shadows, figures, and disjointed details. "As to this salvation, the prophets who prophesied of the grace that would come to you made careful searches and inquiries, seeking to know what person or time the Spirit of Christ within them was indicating as He predicted the sufferings of Christ and the glories to follow" (1 Peter 1:10-11). But as surely as we can sit today with the book of Romans in our hands, the message of salvation in Jesus Christ is plainly revealed to us.

By the "commandment of the eternal God," the book of Romans was sent to us. And with the gospel comes an implied command. Jesus Christ sends the gospel for the purpose of a response. He calls it "the obedience of faith" (1:5). Wherever you are among "all the nations," God commanded the gospel to go to you, and now He commands you to believe. To do so is life eternal and joy unspeakable. But the revelation of the secret mystery, the telling of the gospel, leads to where we began in Romans 1:5. The gospel "leading to the obedience of faith" calls all to repent and believe in Jesus. Entrust yourself to God because "to the only wise God, through Jesus Christ, be the glory forever. Amen."

We have studied through Romans together, and the believing ones emerged together as stronger Christians. Now it invites us back in. Perhaps the Lord will lead you to some of the other sixty-five inspired books before He brings you back here. But unless He calls you home very soon, He will surely bring you back here to Romans before too long. The trouble with the jungle of sin is that we are bound to get our feet dirty in its mud from time to time. Every time we get muddy with sin, and especially if we start to get entangled in the vines of sin, becoming slaves to it, we must run back to Christ, especially as He may be found in the book of Romans.

We must look anew, see the gospel afresh, and remember who we are again. The book of Romans is what every sinner needs. Let us receive it again and again and give it away to everyone we know. Let the good news go forward.

We began this study by asking who and what are "good enough." After all else has been said, "faith comes by hearing, and hearing by the Word of God" (Romans 10:17). God has revealed in His Word that He is good. He is good enough to judge sin. Moreover, He is good enough to save sinners. By contrast, we are not good enough to stand before God or to save ourselves. Our only hope is in a good God who promised "the just shall live by faith" (Romans 1:17). When we trust in Jesus Christ, God declares us "righteous," or "good," enables us to see ourselves as good, teaches us to trust our good sovereign God, guides us to walk by good principles, and firmly establishes us in the good. By the Word of God, especially the book of Romans, we become "wise in what is good and innocent in what is evil" (Romans 16:19).

About the Author

Jeff Kliewer resides in New Jersey with his wife and children. He graduated from Dallas Theological Seminary with a Masters in Cross-Cultural Ministry. Since 2004, he has worked as a missionary to Philadelphia, where he has worked to build up churches. Jeff's life ambition is to know Christ and to make Him known.

Made in the USA
Middletown, DE
26 October 2015